The Airplane

GREAT INVENTIONS

The Airplane

HAROLD FABER

Marshall Cavendish
Benchmark
New York

Marshall Cavendish Benchmark
99 White Plains Road
Tarrytown, NY 10591-9001
www.marshallcavendish.us

Library of Congress Cataloging-in-Publication Data

Faber, Harold.
Airplane / by Harold Faber.
p. cm. — (Great inventions)
Includes bibliographical references and index.
ISBN 0-7614-1876-8
1. Airplanes—Juvenile literature. I. Title. II. Series: Great inventions
(Benchmark Books (Firm))

TL547.F33 2005
629.133'34—dc22
2004022107

Series design by Sonia Chaghatzbanian

Photo research by Candlepants, Inc.

Cover photo: Getty/Taxi/Benjamin Shearn

The photographs in this book are used by permission and through the courtesy of: *Corbis:*
Bettmann, 2, 26, 44, 52-53, 64, 70, 72-73, 74, 79, 101; Museum of Flight, 50; Underwood & Under-
wood, 62; Minnesota Historical Society, 66; Hulton-Deutsch Collection, 69; Benjamin Rondel, 94;
Reuters, 96; Digital Image 1996, original image courtesy of NASA, 98; Philip Wallick, 102. *Art
Resource, NY:* Snark, 8, 17; Image Select, 12; Scala, 14. *Getty Images/Hulton Archive:* 19, 22-23,
30, 43, 56, 59, 77, 82, 86, 89, 91. *Photo Researchers, Inc.:* Mary Evans Picture Library, 33; U.S.
Library of Congress, 36, 106-107; Scaled Composites, 105.

Printed in China

1 3 5 6 4 2

CONTENTS

The Airplane

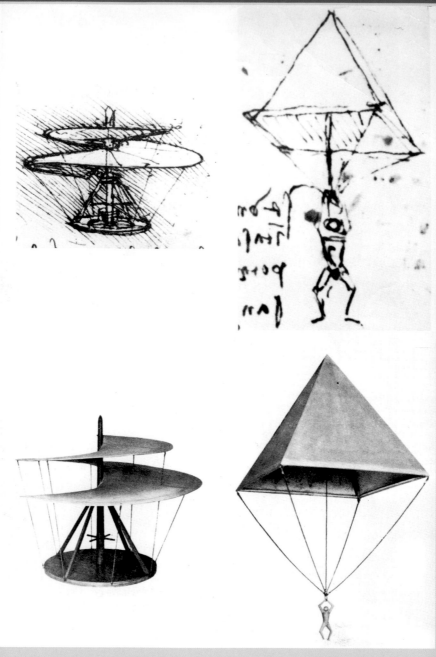

PEOPLE HAD LONG BEEN CAPTIVATED BY THE POSSIBILITY OF FLIGHT. LEONARDO DA VINCI WAS JUST ONE OF MANY VISIONARIES WHO DREAMED OF HUMANS TAKING TO THE SKY. HERE, HIS DRAWINGS FROM THE FIFTEENTH CENTURY ANTICIPATE, CENTURIES IN ADVANCE, THE PARACHUTE AND A SIMPLE, ALBEIT FANCIFUL, FLYING MACHINE.

Introduction

We can pinpoint the precise moment the modern age of aviation was born. At 10:35 on the morning of December 17, 1903, on the sand dunes of Kitty Hawk, North Carolina, Wilbur and Orville Wright made the first powered flight of a heavier-than-air flying machine piloted by a man.

That first flight lasted only 12 seconds and covered only 120 feet (36.6 meters). Not satisfied, the Wright brothers made three more flights that day, the last one covering 852 feet (260 meters) in just 59 seconds. Those short flights began a remarkable era of aviation that opened up the entire world, making once far-distant places accessible to people everywhere.

In a little more than a hundred years, men and women have flown to all corners of the earth and deep into space. Flying has become commonplace for businesspeople, families, and tourists, just as much a part of our daily lives as automobiles, buses, and railroads. It would be hard to imagine working or traveling today if airplanes were not readily available.

The airplane has dramatically changed not only transportation, but commerce, communications, and warfare as well. It has given rise to a huge industry employing large numbers of people, including not just pilots but mechanics, baggage loaders, flight attendants, weather observers, ticket agents, air controllers, instructors, and government regulators.

It is hard to imagine a world without airplanes—when it took a week to cross the Atlantic Ocean by ship instead of the seven hours it takes today, or three days on a train to visit a relative across the continent instead of a speedy six hours. Airplanes have indeed made our world smaller, bringing nations and their peoples closer together than ever before.

Air travel has also opened the door to perhaps the greatest adventure of all—the age of space exploration when voyages to far-distant planets and the stars will become possible. Men have already stepped on the moon. We have landed robot explorers on Mars and are preparing to send astronauts there. We have sent unmanned probes to gather data from other planets and out to the faraway stars. How long will it take for real people to duplicate the feats of men and women in science fiction and television adventure epics who have conquered time and space? Perhaps in your lifetime.

Meanwhile, back on Earth, we enjoy the benefits of air travel, which far outweigh the drawbacks. We have learned to live with airplanes although we complain about the noise of planes flying overhead, air pollution from jet exhaust, crowded airports, flight delays, cramped seating, and the cost of flying. But in the modern world, we cannot do without the airplane. It is just as important as the telephone, the automobile, the radio, the television, the computer, and the food we eat.

The story of this modern marvel is a fascinating one. Above all, it is the tale of men and women who invented airplanes, flew them, and made them into the wonderful instruments that have enhanced the quality of modern life.

NOT QUITE A FLYING CARPET, THE PERSIANS CONJURED THIS IMAGINATIVE MEANS OF ACHIEVING FLIGHT USING TRAINED EAGLES. THE BIRDS WERE GOADED ALONG BY PIECES OF MEAT SUSPENDED FROM THE VEHICLE.

Early Days

People have dreamed of flying through the air ever since primitive men and women first looked into the sky and observed the clouds drifting by and birds circling effortlessly overhead. Almost every ancient culture records legends of flight, usually by gods and kings because such marvelous achievements could be made only by the lofty and elite, not by ordinary men and women.

According to legend, thousands of years ago, the Chinese emperor Shun put on the "clothes" of a bird to fly away and escape captivity.

In ancient Persia, they said that King Kai Kawus used four eagles, stretching for pieces of meat held just beyond their beaks, to draw his throne through the air.

In early Egypt, the winged goddess Isis was carved in stone on the sarcophagus of Rameses III.

The ancient Greeks in their tales of the gods on Mount Olympus endowed them with the ability to fly. The Greek sun god Helios rose in the morning, traveling through the sky in a chariot drawn by four horses before disappearing in the west each evening. Eros, the god of love, flew with golden wings, which sometimes fluttered like a bird. Hermes carried the messages of the gods as rapidly as the wind, propelled by the winged sandals on his feet.

THIS EARLY-SEVENTEENTH-CENTURY PAINTING CAPTURES THE ESCAPE OF ICARUS AND DAEDALUS AND THE TRAGIC END THE AMBITIOUS AND HEADSTRONG BOY FACED.

The Greek legends also gave the gift of flight to a few mortals. Ganymede, described as the most beautiful of all men, flew to the top of Mount Olympus with the aid of an eagle. Perseus, a son of Zeus—the mightiest of all the Greek gods—soared on the flying horse Pegasus after cutting off the snake-covered head of Medusa.

Perhaps the most enduring Greek legend is the story of Daedalus of Athens and his son, Icarus. Daedalus, a craftsman, architect, and engineer hired by Minos, the king of Crete, built a special dwelling to house the Minotaur, a terrible monster with the head of a bull, the body of a man, and an appetite for humans. Every year, Minos forced the city of Athens to send him seven maidens and seven youths as sacrifices to the Minotaur. To keep the youths—and the Minotaur—from escaping, Daedalus built a maze of winding passages so complicated that once inside, it was impossible to get out.

Pleased with his labyrinth, Minos, reluctant to let Daedalus return home, gave him a magnificent workshop, but refused him permission to leave. An independent spirit, Daedalus devised a means of escaping his gilded prison—if he could not leave by ship, he would go by air, just like a bird. He constructed wings made of feathers and wax for himself and Icarus.

When they were ready to leave, Daedalus warned his son not to fly too close to the sun, since it would melt the wax and would cause him to fall into the ocean. Then he and Icarus jumped off a tower and began to fly in the direction of Athens, sailing gently through the air. The flight was so exhilirating that Icarus experimented, soaring high into the sky. But he made a fatal mistake. Not heeding his father's warning, he flew too high, and the sun's rays melted the wax on his wings. Icarus plunged, crashed into the ocean, and drowned. Daedalus circled the area but could see no sign of his son. Distraught, he flew to Athens, mourning a son who would not listen.

The dream of flying did not die with the legends. But it took many centuries before the dream turned into reality.

One of the dreamers was Leonardo da Vinci (1452–1519), the great Italian painter, military engineer, and inventor. He never achieved flight, but his notebooks show that he thought of doing so sometime around the year 1500, although we do not know the exact date. In his notebooks, he drew about 150 sketches of primitive helicopters, a flying machine with flapping birdlike wings, and even a parachute. There is no evidence that he ever tried to build any of them.

It was more than 250 years later before a man rose into the air in a machine for the first time. It happened in France in 1783. The inventors of the first man-made flying machine, a balloon, were the Montgolfier brothers, sons of a prosperous papermaker in Annonay, a small town near Lyon. Joseph, the older, was born in 1740; Étienne, the younger, in 1745. They began to experiment with paper balloons filled with hot air in 1782.

A public demonstration of their balloon took place on June 5, 1783, in the Annonay marketplace. The Montgolfiers had constructed a globe made of three thin layers of paper, 35 feet (10.7 meters) in diameter, with an open mouth at the bottom. They burned straw below the opening, producing heated air which is lighter than normal air. As the heated air filled the paper globe, the balloon lifted, ascending 3,000 feet (915 meters). It floated for a mile and a half (2.4 kilometers) before landing in a nearby vineyard.

When news of the flight reached Paris, the French Academy of Sciences invited the Montgolfiers to demonstrate their new balloon there. Before they could do so, another experimenter, Jacques Charles, duplicated their feat, using a different method. In August he filled a smaller balloon, only 13 feet (4 meters) in diameter, with hydrogen, the lightest gas. This took place on the Champ de Mars, now the site of the Eiffel Tower, in Paris. His balloon rose quickly into the air and flew 15 miles (24.2 kilometers) before it came down.

But an even bigger aviation event in France that year was a demonstration by the Montgolfier brothers at Versailles, the palace of King Louis XV1, on September 19, 1783. They painted their balloon a royal blue to honor the king and attached a basket to it containing a sheep, a rooster, and a duck to find out if the air above was safe to breathe. The balloon soared into the sky for eight minutes before it drifted to the ground, with the animals alive and well.

The next step was to see if a man could go up in a balloon and come down safely. The Montgolfiers constructed another giant balloon, with a large wicker basket suspended beneath it. On November 21, 1783, Jean-Francois Pilatre de Rozier, a young doctor from Metz, and the Mar-

TO THE DELIGHT AND AMAZEMENT OF THE ASSEMBLED CROWD, THE MONTGOLFIER BROTHERS STEP OUT OF THEIR BALLOON, UNSCATHED.

quis Francois d'Arlandes, a soldier, climbed in. They started a small fire in a brazier on the floor of the basket, burning straw to heat air to fill the balloon. They flew for 25 minutes, covering 5 miles (8 kilometers) across Paris before they came down safely. It was the first flight of a manned aircraft in history.

But balloon flight had a serious flaw. Balloons were passive, controlled by the winds and not the passengers onboard. Nevertheless, riding in balloons became popular in Europe. Many daring young men took hazardous trips—across the English Channel, above the Alps, from London to Germany—all going wherever the winds took them. It occurred to some that if power could be added to a balloon, it could be steered midflight. The idea led several years later to the invention of the dirigible—a rigid football-shaped balloon, with a compartment fastened beneath it for carrying passengers and an engine.

It took 120 years of trial and error—from 1783 to 1903—before the first successful flight of a heavier-than-air machine. In the nineteenth century, scientists, engineers, and amateurs began to experiment with gliders, which do not need power, as well as powered flying machines. It was also a century of great advances in other forms of transportation. Steamships, railroads, and automobiles were developed during this time as well.

Even though a practical steam engine had been improved in the late 1760s by James Watt in England, it was not used for locomotion until later. Robert Fulton demonstrated the first commercial steamboat, the *Clermont,* on the Hudson River in New York State in 1807. In 1815 in England, George Stephenson built the first steam locomotive, triggering an era of railroad construction in Europe and America. In 1819 the first steam-powered oceangoing ship, the *Savannah,* crossed the Atlantic from Savannah, Georgia, to Liverpool, England, in twenty-nine days. Gradually steamboats began to replace sailing ships. Late in the century, some early automobile pioneers also used steam engines to propel their vehicles.

Meanwhile, airplane pioneers worked on powerless flight. One of the

THE GERMAN INVENTOR AND AERONAUTICAL ENGINEER OTTO LILIENTHAL COMPLETED HIS FIRST SUCCESSFUL FLIGHT IN 1891. HERE HE GLIDES FROM A HILL IN LICHTERFELDE, NEAR BERLIN.

Zeppelins

Even before the American experiments, several Europeans were trying to fly lighter-than-air vehicles.

In 1852 one early experimenter, a Frenchman named Henri Giffard attached a 3-horsepower steam engine to a cigar-shaped, hydrogen-filled balloon. Although he flew 17 miles (27.4 kilometers) at a rate of about 5 miles (8 kilometers) per hour, his subsequent efforts failed, largely because the weight of the engine made such flight impracticable.

Almost fifty years later, in 1898, Alberto Santos-Dumont, a rich Brazilian living in Paris, who dabbled in building and riding gasoline-powered motorcycles and balloons, decided to combine them. He attached the small engine of one of his motorcycles to a balloon, resulting in the creation of a primitive dirigible. After several accidents, he flew over the city of Paris successfully to the admiration of the French people.

But it was in Germany that the dirigible became commercially possible, due to the efforts of Count Ferdinand von Zeppelin, a former cavalry officer who became an inventor. He built his first airship, the LZ-1—a giant dirigible 450 feet (137.2 meters) long—in 1900. On its first flight, it stayed in the air 18 minutes. Zeppelin improved his airship, and his LZ-3 flew for hours. In 1909 a group of his backers formed the German Aerial Transport Company, the world's first company designed to carry passengers for a profit in any airborne craft. But before commercial service could begin, World War I started, and the dirigible became a military and not a civilian aircraft.

earliest experimenters was Sir George Cayley (1773–1857), an Englishman with an interest in the principles of flying gliders. Over a period of fifty years, he varied the shape of his gliders' wings, measuring their lifting capacity and their resistance to air. He published his results in scientific papers as early as 1809, with figures showing the exact measurements.

Cayley tested gliders with various wing structures as well. In 1853 he built a large glider that carried his coachman about 500 feet (152.5 meters) across a narrow valley. When the glider landed safely, the coachman is reported to have said, "Please, Sir George, I wish to give notice. I was hired to drive and not to fly." Cayley died in 1857, but he left behind a series of scientific papers on wing structure and flight that others subsequently studied. Because of his work, he is sometimes called the father of aeronautics.

In the years that followed, many air pioneers experimented with machines of various designs. In Germany the most prominent was Otto Lilienthal (1848–1896). An engineer and soldier who fought in the Franco-Prussian War of 1870, he returned to Germany, where he built a factory. In his spare time, he studied how birds fly. In 1889 he published a book which, in translation, was titled *Bird Flight as the Basis of Aviation.*

Lilienthal eventually turned theory into practice, building gliders made of wood. He constructed a conical hill 50 feet (15.2 meters) high near his home so that he could take off in any direction by running downhill, no matter which way the wind blew. His gliders were big enough to carry him, but they had no controls; he steered by moving his body and legs. Between 1891 and 1896, he made more than two thousand glider flights, some of them as far as 1,000 feet (305 meters).

From his observation of birds that soared by flapping their wings, he thought that he could duplicate the motion by flapping his glider's wing tips. But before he could try, a tragic accident ended his career. In 1896 a sudden gust of wind upset his glider, and he fell to the ground, fatally injured. Still, his work influenced other air pioneers everywhere.

OCTAVE CHANUTE WAS A PIONEER IN THE CONCEPTION AND CONSTRUCTION OF GLIDERS. HE AND HIS ASSISTANT, AUGUSTUS HERRING, FOUND THE DUNES OF LAKE MICHIGAN THE IDEAL LOCATION FOR TESTING THEIR CREATIONS.

Near the end of the nineteenth century, many experimenters turned to steam power, despite the weight of steam engines, as the answer to the problem of sustained flight. In France in 1890, an electrical engineer named Clement Ader (1841–1926) built a lightweight steam engine specifically for a flying machine. In a test flight, it took off, rising to an altitude of about 8 inches (20.3 centimeters), and flew for about 160 feet (48.8 meters) before descending.

In England the inventor of the machine gun, Sir Hiram Maxim (1840–1916), American born but later a British subject, tried his hand at building his own steam-powered flying machine. It was big, 126 feet (38.4 meters) long, with wings of about 110 feet (33.5 meters), weighing 8,000 pounds (3,632 kilograms). Its forward motion was provided by two propellers driven by a huge steam engine that produced 360 horsepower. Sir Hiram tested his machine in 1894, placing himself and two other passengers aboard. The machine ran briefly along a wooden rail, but one of its wheels caught on the rail, causing a crash. Unhurt, he turned off the engine. "Propulsion and lifting are solved problems," he said, even though his machine had not lifted off the ground. "The rest is a mere matter of time."

The next steps toward flight were taken in the United States. Three teams of Americans were working independently on the problems of flying at roughly the same time in the 1890s.

Octave Chanute, a civil engineer and the author of *Progress in Flying Machines,* published in 1894, designed and flew gliders with the assistance of Augustus Herring, another engineer, on the south side of Lake Michigan near Chicago.

Chanute (1832–1910), born in Paris, had immigrated to the United States with his family when he was a boy. After studying civil engineering, he specialized in building bridges and rose to the post of chief engineer of the Erie Railroad. Extensive reading about aviation piqued his curiosity, so he decided to build gliders, using his knowledge of bridge building to increase their structural strength. On the dunes of Lake Michigan, Herring flew one of Chanute's gliders 360 feet (109.7 meters) in 14 seconds.

But Chanute never progressed beyond simple glider flight to a fully powered flying machine.

A second pioneer, Samuel P. Langley (1834–1906), the secretary of the Smithsonian Institution, did. He and his aides constructed and flew model airplanes before he attempted to fly a steam-powered craft he called an Aerodrome (from the Greek meaning "air runner"). By 1896 he had perfected a 14-foot (4.3-meter) steam-driven model that flew for three-quarters of a mile (1.2 kilometers) at an altitude of between 80 and 100 feet (24.4 and 30.5 meters) before it fell, its fuel exhausted.

Aided by a grant of $50,000 from the Department of War, Langley's next step was to construct a full-scale plane capable of carrying a man. By this time, Langley had realized that a steam engine would be too heavy for a flying machine. So he and his assistant, Charles M. Manley, hired a New York engine builder, Stephen Balzer, to design a small internal-combustion engine.

In 1902 Balzer produced an engine weighing only 125 pounds (56.7 kilograms), a major accomplishment. Langley and Manley installed it on a plane they launched from a catapult mounted on a houseboat in the Potomac River. With Manley at the controls, the plane, its twin propellers biting into the air, sped forward. Instead of rising into the air, though, it crashed into the river below and was destroyed. Langley and Manley tried again, with a rebuilt plane. But once again, the catapult shot the plane forward; and instead of flying, it fell into the river—another failure.

Meanwhile, in Dayton, Ohio, an unlikely pair of brothers, Orville and Wilbur Wright, who ran a bicycle repair and sales service, were experimenting with gliders and engines.

ORVILLE (LEFT) AND WILBUR WRIGHT WOULD LEAVE AN INDELIBLE MARK ON THE WORLD WITH THEIR PIONEERING WORK IN AVIATION.

The Wright Brothers

How did two bicycle mechanics who didn't even graduate from high school succeed in inventing the airplane, while skilled engineers and scientists from around the world failed?

To get the answer, one must examine the life and times of Wilbur and Orville Wright. They grew up in the last half of the nineteenth century, a time of flourishing inventive genius as well as industrial growth in the United States following the end of the Civil War. Look at this short list of inventions from that period:

typewriter, Christopher Sholes, 1868
telephone, Alexander Graham Bell, 1876
phonograph, Thomas Alva Edison, 1877
electric lights, Edison, 1879
gasoline-powered automobile, George B. Selden, 1879
dishwasher, Josephine Cochrane, 1886
camera, George Eastman, 1888
alternating-current electric motor, Nikola Tesla, 1888
aluminum manufacturing, Charles Hall, 1889
zipper, Whitcomb Judson, 1893
motion-picture camera, Edison, 1893

It was almost as if innovation was in the air as the Wright boys came of age in the Midwest. Wilbur, the older of the pair, was born on April 16, 1867, in Millville, Indiana. His younger brother, Orville, was born in Dayton, Ohio, on August 19, 1871. Their father, Milton Wright, was a minister for the United Brethren in Christ Church, editor of its newspaper, and later a bishop. Their mother, Susan, took care of a family of five children. They had two older brothers, Reuchlin and Lorin, and a younger sister, Katharine. By all accounts, it was a close-knit, happy household. Although he traveled a lot as a bishop, Milton Wright always brought home toys for the children because he believed they had an educational value. The boys never forgot one present in particular, a toy helicopter, which possibly gave them their first notion that they could fly, too.

Wilbur had a nickname, Ullam, a variation of the German for William. Orville was called Bubbo or Bubs, the way Wilbur mispronounced his brother's name when he was born. Once Wilbur wrote, "From the time we were little children, my brother Orville and myself lived together, played together, worked together, and, in fact, thought together." Wilbur, a devoted reader, would have graduated from high school with high grades, but his family moved during his senior year. Orville, on the other hand, was an ordinary student who quit school before his senior year to start a printing business, using a press he built himself.

The first time the pair referred to themselves as the Wright brothers was in 1889, when they printed their own weekly community newspaper, the *West Side News.* Wilbur served as the editor and Orville as the publisher. In the next few years, when riding bicycles had become a fad, they took it up as a hobby. Soon they began to repair their friends' bicycles and then, as they became expert mechanics, they went into the repair business. By 1896 they were manufacturing and selling bicycles as well.

That year proved to be a turning point in their lives. Wilbur was twenty-nine years old and Orville twenty-five. After Orville recovered from a bout of typhoid fever, Wilbur read to him about something new, the growing interest all over the world in gliding. They were particularly fascinated by the story of Lilienthal, who died in a glider crash in Germany that same year, and in the test flights of Chanute and Langley in the United States. After writing to the Smithsonian Institution asking for literature on gliders and flying, they carefully read what they received. Wilbur later wrote, "When we came to examine these books, we were astonished to learn what an immense amount of time and money had been expended in futile attempts to solve the problem of human flight."

The failures of more prominent experimenters did not deter the Wrights. Not only did they yearn to fly, they had the time and the money to pursue their ambition. Neither Wilbur nor Orville ever married. After their mother died in 1889, they lived at home in Dayton with their father and their sister, Katharine, a graduate of Oberlin College and a high school teacher of English and Latin, who ran the household. Their bicycle shop prospered, giving them enough money to buy equipment and conduct their aviation experiments.

From their reading, the Wrights concluded that there were three essential elements to flying: wings to provide lift, a lightweight engine to provide enough power to propel the plane forward, and a means to control the airplane in the air. The early experimenters, particularly Lilienthal and Langley, had almost solved the first element—wings—but not the second and third—power and control. From their experience with bicycles, the Wrights knew that steering was the key to successful riding. Obviously in the three-dimensional atmosphere, it was even more important to control the movements of an airplane.

Even though they were not trained scientists, the Wright brothers used scientific methods to observe, investigate, test, and build their aircraft, making adjustments and changes as they went along. Deciding to test a glider big enough to hold a man where the winds were strong and consistent enough to lift it off the ground, they wrote to the Weather Bureau in Washington, D.C., asking for a list of windy places. The Outer

THE HIGH-FLYING WILBUR WRIGHT SOARS IN HIS WRIGHT NUMBER 1 GLIDER AT KILL DEVIL HILL NEAR KITTY HAWK, NORTH CAROLINA.

Banks of North Carolina, a group of long narrow islands with the Atlantic Ocean to the east and Albermarle Sound to the west, seemed the most promising.

They made their first trip to Kitty Hawk, a hamlet on the Outer Banks consisting of a post office and a few homes, in 1900. The local residents, most of whom worked at the nearby Kill Devil Hill Lifesaving Station, greeted them warmly and helped them with their living arrangements and experiments. After they put up a tent to live in and a shed to house their machine, their test flights began. The results showed that the wingspan of their glider, 17 feet (5.2 meters), was not big enough to provide the necessary lift. So they returned to Dayton for more experiments. A year later they were back in Kitty Hawk with a larger craft. Once more they found that the wings were insufficient to provide enough lift.

Back in Dayton, they constructed a small wind tunnel of wood, measuring 6 feet (1.8 meters) long and 16 inches square (103.2 square centimeters), to test various wing constructions for lift and resistance to wind. With a fan providing a wind velocity of 27 miles (43.5 kilometers) per hour, they patiently tested more than two hundred miniature wing surfaces before concluding that the aircraft's wings had to be longer and thinner. Returning to the Outer Banks, they adapted their 1902 model with new wings and a movable rudder that permitted them to control turns. But it was still only a glider subject to the vagaries of the wind.

To fly independent of the wind, they needed power to propel their machine. Steam engines proved much too heavy, so they looked to the new internal-combustion engines that used gasoline as fuel. Many pioneering auto manufacturers built such engines, but all those engines were much too heavy, as well. So, back in their Dayton bicycle shop, with the help of an experienced mechanic who was their assistant, Charles E. Taylor, they built a small engine of their own design. With four cylinders, it weighed 180 pounds (81.6 kilograms) and produced 12 horsepower, which they thought would be enough to propel their new craft.

Paving the Way

One more major step remained before they could test it—propellers that could use the engine's power to move the airplane forward. They could find no one who had designed propellers for airplanes. Undaunted, they decided to make their own. It took them three months of calculations, then carving wood with hand tools and testing before they had a propeller they thought sufficient for the job.

Before they took their new machine to Kitty Hawk, confident that it would fly, they applied for a patent, on March 23, 1903. In the application, they said:

> Be it known that we, Orville and Wilbur Wright, citizens of the United States, residing in the city of Dayton, county of Montgomery, and State of Ohio, have invented certain new and useful Improvements in Flying Machines. . . .
>
> Our invention relates to that class of flying machines in which the weight is sustained by the reactions resulting when one or more aeroplanes [wings] are moved through the air edgewise at a small angle of incidence either by the application of mechanical power or by the utilization of the force of gravity.

But the U.S. Patent Office rejected their application. It said the drawings were inadequate and the description too vague. But the Patent Office had one helpful suggestion: that the Wrights hire a patent attorney to help them, which they did.

In September 1903 they took their new plane to Kitty Hawk and began a series of test flights at nearby Kill Devil Hill. The plane looked like

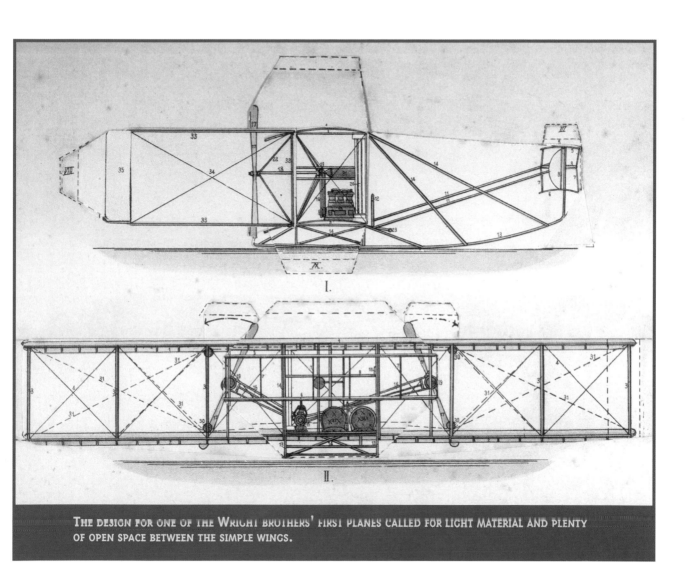

I.

II.

THE DESIGN FOR ONE OF THE WRIGHT BROTHERS' FIRST PLANES CALLED FOR LIGHT MATERIAL AND PLENTY OF OPEN SPACE BETWEEN THE SIMPLE WINGS.

a huge glider but there was an important difference—the addition of an engine. Unlike modern airplanes, which are longer than they are wide, the Wright machine was much wider than long. Here are its dimensions:

Wingspan: 40 feet 4 inches (12.3 meters)
Length: 21 feet (6.4 meters)
Height: 8 feet 3 inches (2.52 meters)
Weight, empty: 605 pounds (274.7 kilograms)
Engine: gasoline, 12 horsepower

Its two wings were constructed of wood—spruce and ash—and covered with muslin. In the center of the lower wing was a simple wooden cradle where the pilot could lie facedown. A four-cylinder engine on the wing to his right was connected via bicycle chains to the two propellers, each 8 feet (2.4 meters) in diameter, mounted in the rear of the machine. Above him to his left, a gasoline tank held a small amount of fuel with a gravity flow line to the engine. Together the plane, the engine, and the pilot weighed 750 pounds (341 kilograms). They called their machine the Flyer although it had not yet flown.

To provide the initial lift into the air, the plane, which had no wheels, slid down a 60-foot (18.3-meter) wooden launching rail built on the slope of the sand dunes while the engine provided the power to propel the craft forward and up. The pilot could control the flight, in a primitive fashion, in two ways. First, if he shifted his hips, the cradle would move to the right or left, pulling wires that bent the ends of the wings slightly and made it easier to turn. Second, if he pulled a lever to his left, the pilot would initiate an up-and-down movement of small winglike elevators mounted in front of him, which helped control the vertical motion of the plane.

On December 14, Wilbur won a coin toss with his brother to see who would be first to test their creation. He climbed into the plane, which, after sliding down the launching rail with the engine purring away, rose a few feet into the air for about 3 seconds, then fell to the sand. But they were not discouraged. On the contrary, Wilbur said, "The power is ample, and but for a trifling error due to lack of experience with this machine and this method of starting, the machine would have undoubtedly flown beautifully. There is now no question of final success."

Three days later, on December 17, the plane had been repaired, and they were ready to try again. It was a cold day, with the wind blowing between 21 and 27 miles (33.8 and 43.5 kilometers) per hour, strong enough so that they could launch from level ground rather than down a hill. This time it was Orville's turn to try to fly. Five men, some of whom had helped the Wrights prepare—John T. Daniels, Willie S. Dough, and Adam Etheridge of the Kill Devil Hill Lifesaving Station and two neighbors, William C. Brinkley and John T. Moore—were present. Before climbing into the plane, Orville put a box camera on a tripod nearby and asked Daniels to take a picture if the plane lifted off and flew.

At 10:35 in the morning, with Wilbur jogging alongside, the plane slowly gathered speed on the wooden rail, traveling about 7 or 8 miles (11.3 or 12.9 kilometers) per hour into the headwind. It slowly lifted off the rail and rose to a height of about 10 feet (3 meters). In Orville's diary, he wrote:

> The course of the flight up and down was exceedingly erratic, partly because of the gusty air, and partly because of my inexperience in handling this machine. It would rise suddenly to about 10 feet [3 meters] and then as suddenly [when I turned] the rudder, dart for the ground. On one of those darts, it hit the ground. I had been in the air 12 seconds and covered a distance of 120 feet [36.6 meters].

In those 12 seconds, Daniels snapped a picture—the only picture of the first successful flight of a heavier-than-air machine carrying a passenger. Unlike the Langley flight, which had ended in failure nine days before and been witnessed by reporters in Washington, the successful Wright flight was made with no press present—and, therefore,

A PHOTOGRAPH OF AN HISTORIC DAY—DECEMBER 17, 1903—AS HUMANS ACHIEVE POWERED FLIGHT FOR THE FIRST TIME. ORVILLE IS AT THE CONTROLS, AS WILBUR JOGS ALONGSIDE.

no publicity. The only witnesses to the historic flight were Daniels and the four other men from the area. Orville later wrote:

> This flight lasted only 12 seconds, but it was nevertheless the first in the history of the world in which a machine carrying a man had raised itself by its own power into the air in full flight, had sailed forward without reduction of speed, and had finally landed at a point as high as that from which it had started.

It was Wilbur's turn next. He got into the plane, and once again it was successfully launched. This time he flew about 195 feet (59.4 meters). On a third flight, Orville tried again, flying a little farther, about 200 feet (61 meters). With each successive flight, they were learning how to control their new machine. On their fourth attempt that day, Wilbur got into the flying machine at about noon. Here is how Orville described that flight:

> The machine started off with its ups and downs as it has before but by the time he had gone four hundred feet [122 meters] he had it under much better control, and traveling on a fairly even course. It was proceeding in this manner until it reached a small hummock out about 800 feet [244 meters] from the starting ways, when it began pitching again and suddenly darted into the ground. The distance over the ground was 852 feet [259.7 meters] in 59 seconds.

The Wrights knew what they had accomplished—they had built an airplane that could actually fly. Before they carried the plane back to its hangar, though, a sudden gust of wind struck it, turned it over, and damaged it so severely that it could not be flown again. Later that day, Orville walked 4 miles (6.4 kilometers) to the nearest telegraph office and sent a message to his father in Dayton.

> Bishop M. Wright
>
> Success four flights Thursday morning all against twenty-one mile [33.8-kilometer] wind started from level with engine power alone average speed through air thirty-one miles [50 kilometers] longest 57 seconds inform press home Christmas.
>
> Oreveille Wright

Another Inventor?

Not everybody accepts the Wrights as the inventors of the airplane. In Brazil, credit is given to Alberto Santos-Dumont (1873–1932), the son of a rich Brazilian coffee grower, who lived in Paris and experimented with flying machines. In 1901 he flew a primitive lighter-than-air dirigible around the Eiffel Tower in Paris. In 1906, three years after the Wrights' flight, Santos-Dumont demonstrated in public his heavier-than-air flying machine, which had box kites as wings and was powered by an automobile engine. He made three short flights and was acclaimed in Europe as the first man to fly (because they had not heard of the Wrights at that time).

In Brazil, the city of Santos-Dumont, named in his honor, greets visitors with a billboard that reads, "Welcome to the Land of the Father of Aviation." His advocates say that he is truly the inventor of the airplane because he flew his machine before the public—unlike the Wrights, who made their flights in virtual secrecy. Nevertheless, aviation historians still regard the Wrights as the inventors of the airplane, but give Santos-Dumont credit for making the first airplane flights in Europe.

In the transmission, the telegram contained two errors—the actual time was 59 seconds and, of course, Orville's name was misspelled. Bishop Wright informed the Associated Press representative in Dayton, who said, "Fifty-seven seconds, heh? If it had been 57 minutes, then it might have been a news item." And so no news story about the flight was dispatched that day from Dayton.

News of the flight leaked out, though. Informed of Orville's message by a telegraph operator, the *Virginian-Pilot*, the leading newspaper in Norfolk, printed a garbled account of the day's events on its front page. But the nation's press, rather than being impressed by the Wrights' historic accomplishment, largely ignored it. Editors were skeptical because there had been so many earlier stories about successful flights that had turned out to be false. And so the Wrights returned to Dayton, while the world outside paid little attention to them and their revolutionary invention.

IN 1909 A FARMER IN PAU, FRANCE, PAUSES FROM HIS WORK IN THE HAY FIELDS TO WITNESS WHAT MAY HAVE BEEN THE STARTLING SIGHT OF WILBUR WRIGHT FLYING BY IN HIS DISTINCTIVE BIPLANE.

Growth and Development

Back in Dayton, the Wrights tinkered with their Flyer, building larger models with improved methods of control. With a more powerful engine, they no longer needed a headwind to lift into the air. Instead they took off from a nearby level cow pasture called Huffman Prairie, about 6 miles (9.7 kilometers) out of town. By October 1904 they had made about one hundred flights in their new Flyer 2. In 1905 their Flyer 3 stayed in the air for 38 minutes and covered more than 24 miles (38.6 kilometers).

Now the challenge was one of marketing. Who would buy their airplane and others like it that they could manufacture? Surprisingly, more interest was shown by foreign countries than by the United States. A British delegation came to inspect the Wrights' invention, and the French bought an option to purchase one. But not the United States. The army, which years ago had paid Langley $50,000 to perform flight experiments, rejected offers by the Wrights to demonstrate their plane.

But the Wrights were patient. They knew they had created a valuable commodity and were not going to sell the plane or the patent rights too cheaply. On May 22, 1906, the U.S. Patent Office granted them patent number 821,393, the first patent ever issued for an airplane.

Meanwhile, in an unusual coincidence, another bicycle mechanic, Glenn Curtiss (1878–1930), also became a flight pioneer. Curtiss lived in Hammondsport, on the southern end of Lake Keuka, one of New York's Finger Lakes. In 1900 he opened a bicycle shop and soon began to manufacture and race them. From there it was a short step from manufacturing bicycles to putting engines on them and converting them into motorcycles, which he also built and raced. His vehicles functioned so well that he became the American motorcycle speed record-holder in 1907, traveling 136.36 miles (219.5 kilometers) per hour, thus gaining the unofficial title of "the fastest man in the world."

His skill in producing engines attracted Alexander Graham Bell, the inventor of the telephone, who was also interested in flight. Bell asked Curtiss to build an engine for an experimental plane, which he did. Bell and Curtiss got along so well that they and others formed the Aerial Experiment Association, based in Hammondsport.

As director of experiments for the association, Curtiss spearheaded the manufacture of a plane he designed himself, called the June Bug. Unlike the Wrights' Flyer, which needed to ride along a wooden rail in order to achieve liftoff, the June Bug had wheels which could roll across the ground before it rose. On July 4, 1908, in Hammondsport, before a crowd of several hundred spectators, including reporters, photographers, and a motion-picture cameraman, the June Bug made a well-publicized flight of more than 1 mile (1.6 kilometers) at an altitude of about 20 feet (6.1 meters). With that flight, Curtiss won a Scientific American Trophy, which came with a prize of $2,500.

By 1908 the Wrights and Curtiss were the leading American pioneers in aviation development, working separately and often in conflict. For example, the Wrights, who were quite belligerent in defending their patent rights, sued Curtiss for patent infringement because the June Bug used ailerons on the ends of its wings to control its lateral movements, a device the Wrights believed copied their patented idea of wing warping. After a series of court battles, the Wrights finally won, but they could not control the development and manufacture of airplanes both in the United States and in Europe.

A WRIGHT BROTHERS PLANE CRASHED ON SEPTEMBER 17, 1908, AT FORT MYER, VIRGINIA, INJURING ORVILLE WRIGHT AND KILLING HIS PASSENGER LIEUTENANT THOMAS SELFRIDGE, THE FIRST VICTIM OF AN AVIATION ACCIDENT.

In 1908, five years after their historic first flight, the Wrights finally received public recognition at home and abroad. In the United States, the army accepted their offer to demonstrate their plane for military use. The Wrights also signed a contract with a French company allowing it to manufacture and sell their planes in France. Before proceeding on either project, though, the Wrights made several major improvements. They changed the position of the pilot from lying prone to sitting upright, added a new set of hand levers to control the plane, and built a second seat for a passenger. Wilbur traveled to France to demonstrate the new plane, while Orville stayed behind to perform the tests for the army.

Orville made his first public flight on September 3, 1908, at Fort Myer, Virginia, just outside Washington, D.C. Flying solo, he circled the field, turning effortlessly while the spectators below, according to one witness, "went crazy" with excitement. On the last day of the test, Sep-

LADY LINDY—AMELIA EARHART IS KNOWN AS MUCH FOR HER FLYING PROWESS AS FOR HER MYSTERIOUS DISAPPEARANCE NEAR HOWLAND ISLAND ON JULY 2, 1937.

Women with Wings

As might be expected, women as well as men decided to become pilots as soon as news filtered out about successful airplane flights. In 1910 the Aero Club of France issued its first license to a woman, the Baroness Elise de La Roche, who has been called the world's first female pilot.

Two years later on August 2, 1912, after Harriet Quimby, a freelance journalist, had learned to fly at a school on Long Island, New York, she became the first American woman to gain a pilot's license from the Aero Club of America. She traveled to France and somehow convinced Louis Bleriot to lend her a plane that she flew across the English Channel, becoming the first woman to do so.

She was the first in a long line of pioneering women aviators—Amelia Earhart, the first woman to fly solo across the Atlantic Ocean; Bessie Coleman, the first African-American woman pilot; Jacqueline Cochran, who set many speed records; Valentina Tereshkova, the Russian woman who was the first to orbit the earth in space; and Sally Ride, the first American female astronaut to travel into space.

tember 17, during a flight with an army officer, the plane crashed. The passenger, Lieutenant Thomas Selfridge, was killed, the first recorded fatality in an airplane crash. Orville was badly injured, with a broken leg and several broken ribs, but he eventually recovered.

Back at the controls in 1909, Orville successfully completed the army's requirements, flying 10 miles (16.1 kilometers) in 14 minutes, or just less than 43 miles (69.2 kilometers) per hour. The army formally adopted the Wright plane on August 2, 1909, paying the brothers $30,000, which included the fee of $25,000 plus a bonus of $5,000 for exceeding the required speed. That day could be called the birth date of the U.S. Air Force (even though it was not called that until 1947; before then it was a branch of the army).

Meanwhile in France, Wilbur was flying in triumph. At Le Mans, not far from Paris, he astonished the crowds by his graceful flying, circling the field, making perfect figure eights and graceful turns. The French newspaper *Le Figaro* commented, "It was not merely a success, but a triumph, a conclusive and a decisive victory for aviation, the news of which will revolutionize scientific circles throughout the world."

After Orville and Katharine joined their brother in Europe, the Wrights became celebrities, receiving medals and honors from the press, royalty, and the public. Wilbur accepted the praise modestly. At one dinner in his honor, he remarked, "I only know of one bird, the parrot that can talk, and it doesn't fly very high." When they returned to the United States, they also received many honors and medals from Congress, the Aero Club of America, and the Smithsonian Institution, as well as a parade in their hometown of Dayton.

Wilbur gave residents of New York City their first glimpse of an airplane in flight by flying up the Hudson River from Governors Island to Grant's Tomb as part of the Hudson-Fulton celebration (it was 300 years since Henry Hudson had discovered the river that was named for him and 102 years after Robert Fulton had made the first steamboat voyage on the river aboard the *Clermont*).

In that same year, 1909, Louis Bleriot (1872–1936), another pioneering aviator, made history by becoming the first person to fly across the English Channel. He traveled from Calais, France, to Dover, England, covering 26 miles (41.8 kilometers) in 37 minutes. His flight was one sign of the emergence of France as a leading force in the development of aviation.

France's prominence in aviation became clear in late August 1909, with the first great international air show held in Rheims (sometimes spelled Reims), a small city east of Paris, where virtually every aircraft pioneer, except the Wrights, was present. Henri Farman of France won a prize for endurance, flying for 3 hours. Glenn Curtiss of the United States won the speed prize for flying 43 miles (69.2 kilometers) per hour.

In the years immediately preceding World War I, there was an explosion of public interest in aviation. Both the Wrights and Curtiss opened schools to teach flying. They organized exhibition teams to travel around the country demonstrating airplanes at farm pastures and fairgrounds, where stunt pilots performed daring feats of aerial acrobatics. Separately, the Wrights and Curtiss also organized rival companies to manufacture their airplanes, and all three prospered.

The next several years were a mixture of triumph and tragedy for the Wrights. In late 1909 Wilbur took charge of production at their manufacturing factory in Dayton. In 1910 a judge upheld the Wright patent in their suit against Curtiss, but Curtiss continued to fight them by filing various appeals. In 1912 Wilbur was stricken with typhoid fever and died at the age of forty-five. In 1915 Orville, at the age of forty-four, sold the company to a group of investors for $1.5 million. (And, in an ironic twist, many years later, in 1929, the two rival companies founded by the Wrights and Curtiss merged to form the Curtiss-Wright Company, then and to this day one of the major manufacturers of airplanes and engines.)

One final footnote to the story of the Wright brothers. What happened to the 1903 Flyer?

Visitors to the National Air and Space Museum in Washington, D.C., today will find it as the centerpiece of an exhibit commemorating more than one hundred years of flight. But it took forty-five years for it to reach there.

Despite the success of the Wrights' Flyer and the failure of Langley's Aerodrome, the Smithsonian Institution insisted for years that Langley had succeeded in building "the first aeroplane capable of sustaining free flight with a man." It even put a reconstruction of the Langley machine on display with a label calling it "the first man-made aeroplane in the history of the world capable of sustained free flight."

Orville Wright reacted angrily to what he considered to be an insult to him and his brother. He announced that he would send the Flyer abroad to be displayed at the London Science Museum, and he did so, vowing not to bring it home to the United States until the Smithsonian corrected the record by giving full credit to the Wrights. The feud continued for years, during which Orville received honors and medals from countries all over the world. It ended in 1948 when Orville died, at the age of seventy-seven. The Smithsonian finally yielded. Shortly after ten o'clock on the morning of December 17, 1948, exactly forty-five years after the historic flight, the Smithsonian put the reconstructed original Flyer on display with the following explanation:

THE ORIGINAL WRIGHT BROTHERS AEROPLANE
THE WORLD'S FIRST POWER-DRIVEN
HEAVIER-THAN-AIR MACHINE IN WHICH MAN
MADE FREE, CONTROLLED AND SUSTAINED FLIGHT
INVENTED AND BUILT
BY WILBUR AND ORVILLE WRIGHT
FLOWN BY THEM AT KITTY HAWK, NORTH CAROLINA
DECEMBER 17, 1903

BY ORIGINAL SCIENTIFIC RESEARCH
THE WRIGHT BROTHERS
DISCOVERED THE PRINCIPLES OF HUMAN FLIGHT
AS INVENTORS, BUILDERS, AND FLIERS, THEY
FURTHER DEVELOPED THE AEROPLANE,
TAUGHT MAN TO FLY, AND OPENED
THE ERA OF AVIATION

THOUGH MOST OF THE WORLD WAR I WAS FOUGHT ON THE GROUND, THE ARRIVAL OF THE AIRPLANE CHANGED THE FACE OF WAR FOREVER. HERE, SOLDIERS GATHER AROUND THE WRECKAGE OF A ROYAL AIR FORCE SOPWITH *CAMEL,* DOWNED DURING AERIAL COMBAT IN 1917.

FOUR

World War I

World War I sparked a dramatic growth in interest in the technology of aviation. Once the war started in 1914, it became a clash between the invading Germans and the combined British and French defenders that was decided on the battlefields of eastern France. At the time, airplanes were not considered a major weapon by either side. When hostilities broke out, the Germans had about 450 planes, the British 160, and the French 300. The United States did not enter the war until 1917, when its air effort consisted of 131 officers, 1,000 enlisted men, and 250 aircraft.

In the early days of the war, airplanes were used for observation of enemy forces, but gradually they evolved into fighter planes and bombers, as well. Those early planes were primitive. They could achieve speeds of about 60 to 70 miles (96.6 to 112.7 kilometers) per hour and had open cockpits, usually containing a single seat for the pilot. A few planes were equipped with second cockpits, with the rear one used by an observer who held a bulky camera over the side to take pictures. Obviously, these observer planes were enemy targets. The pilots of fighter planes sent out to shoot them down found it difficult because they had to fly the planes as well as operate rifles or hand guns.

THE FAMED FOKKER TRIWING, THE GERMAN-CREATED MODEL IN WHICH BARON MANFRED VON RICHTHOFEN SHOWCASED HIS TALENTS AS AN AERIAL FIGHTER.

The art of aerial warfare took a dramatic step forward in 1915 when Roland Garros, a French flier, solved that problem. He devised a system of shooting a machine gun through the arc of a propeller protected with steel wedges to deflect outgoing bullets. It was deadly and effective, and Garros became the first ace of the war—shooting down five or more enemy planes. The Germans soon came up with their own solution. They turned to a brilliant young Dutchman, Anthony Fokker, who invented a synchronized system whereby a machine gun could fire its bullets between the turns of a propeller blade—something that still sounds impossible, but it worked.

One of the precocious geniuses of aviation history, Fokker (1890–1939) was born in Java, where his father was a coffee planter. He grew up in Haarlem, the Netherlands, where he showed a great interest in mechanics, engines, and vehicles. By 1910, when he was only twenty years old, he had designed and built his first airplane. He was later invited to Germany, where he set up an aircraft-manufacturing plant. When World War I broke out, he built fighter planes, among them a Fokker triwing, one of the best fighters of the war. When the war ended, Fokker immigrated to the United States, where he became president of the Fokker Aircraft Corporation of America.

Unlike World War II, when bombing was an effective tool of war, during World War I, bombing from the air was sporadic and ineffective. The Germans sent zeppelins on bombing raids over England starting in 1915, but the damage was minimal. Moreover, just as in World War II, instead of demoralizing civilians, bombing raids angered them and hardened their will to resist.

If a pilot was shot down, his plane either burned or crashed, and few walked away from the wreckage.

The most famous World War I pilot was a young German, Baron Manfred von Richthofen (1892–1918), called the Red Baron because his triwinged Fokker plane was painted all red. Even his enemies conceded that he was the greatest aerial fighter of the war; he scored eighty "kills" against Allied planes before he himself was shot down and killed in 1918. The leading French ace, Captain René Fonck, shot down seventy-five German planes; the top English ace, Major Edward Mannock, seventy-three; and the top Canadian ace, Captain William "Billy" Bishop, seventy-two.

Not until April 1918, a year after the United States entered the war, did Americans join the aerial combat. They had spent the previous year training in the United States on JN-4Ds, popularly called Jennies, and in France on French-built Nieuports and Spads. Earlier, a few Americans had enlisted in the *Escadrille Americaine,* or American squadron, and had flown under the French flag. Now the Americans were in France, flying under their own flag, but still using French and English airplanes; no American planes reached Europe during the war.

The two leading American fliers were Captain Eddie Rickenbacker, who shot down twenty-six German aircraft (after the war he operated a commercial airline back home) and Lieutenant Frank Luke, who shot down twenty-one before he was killed in action. They were the only two

American pilots to receive the Medal of Honor for outstanding bravery in battle.

Despite the glamour of the air war, it was really a sideshow to the ground war, more spectacular than effective. But it led to important technical developments in airplane design and manufacture, more powerful engines, new flying techniques, and, more important, the training of tens of thousands of pilots, mechanics, and aircraft construction workers who formed a base for the rapid advances in aviation that lay in store in the years ahead.

AMERICAN AVIATOR CHARLES LINDBERGH POSES IN FULL FLYING REGALIA IN THIS PHOTOGRAPH OF JULY 21, 1925.

"The Lone Eagle"

The most famous aviator of the twentieth century was a young American from Minnesota named Charles A. Lindbergh (1902–1974). He soared into fame in 1927 by making the first solo transatlantic flight between the United States and Europe. Acclaimed abroad and at home, the shy young man became a worldwide symbol of courage and skill.

Lindbergh's rise to fame started in Little Falls, a small city on the Mississippi River in central Minnesota. Born on February 4, 1902, he was named Charles Augustus Lindbergh after his father, a prosperous lawyer and later a member of the House of Representatives in Washington, D.C. His mother, Evangeline Lindbergh, taught science at the local high school. His interest in aviation began when as a boy he would lie on the grass in Little Falls and stare at the sky: "How wonderful it would be, I'd thought, if I had an airplane—wings with which I could fly up to the clouds." Unlike thousands of other kids who had the same daydreams, Lindbergh realized his ambition.

When he was eighteen years old, he entered the University of Wisconsin to study mechanical engineering. He was tall and skinny, 6 feet 2 inches (1.9 meters) in height, weighing only 142 pounds (64.4 kilograms), prompting his fellow students to call him Slim, a nickname that stuck. A poor student, he failed math and chemistry but excelled in the Reserve Officers Training Corps, becoming an expert marksman with both the rifle and pistol. In his sophomore year, he decided to drop out of college and learn to fly. On April 9, 1922, at the age of twenty, he made his first airplane flight at an aviation school in Lincoln, Nebraska. With quick reflexes, Lindbergh proved to be a natural pilot.

After about a year of barnstorming—traveling around the country with another pilot putting on air shows at county fairs and farm fields that featured parachute jumps and wing walking—Lindbergh enlisted in the Army Air Service in 1924. He trained at Brook and Kelly fields in San Antonio, Texas, in a rigorous and disciplined course. Of the 104 men who entered with him, only 19 completed the training, with Lindbergh—the college dropout—the best pilot and top graduate in his class. At the age of twenty-three, he was commissioned as a second lieutenant in the reserves, but there was no place in the small regular army for him. So he took a job in St. Louis, flying airmail between that city and Chicago.

It was in St. Louis in early 1927 that the dream of flying across the Atlantic Ocean first took shape for him. Lindbergh and many other fliers in the United States and Europe were attracted by a prize of $25,000 offered by Raymond Orteig, a New York hotel owner, to "the first aviator of any allied country crossing the Atlantic in one flight, from Paris to New York or New York to Paris." Even though he had only five years of flying experience, Lindbergh was confident that he could do it—if he had financial backers and the right plane.

Eight years earlier, in 1919, two separate military teams, one American and one British—had crossed the Atlantic Ocean but in a manner that did not really meet Orteig's definition of a nonstop transatlantic flight.

On May 8, 1919, Lieutenant Commander Albert C. Read (1887–1967) led a U.S. Navy crew of five that took off from Rockaway, New York, aboard a four-engined Curtiss flying boat, destined for England. It made several stops along the way; at Nova Scotia, Newfoundland; the Azores, Portugal; and finally Plymouth, England, on May 31. The total flying time was 57 hours 16 minutes. Even though it was done in stages, it was

A famous pairing—Charles Lindbergh poses beside the *Spirit of St. Louis*, the plane that guided him safely across the Atlantic Ocean.

the first flight of any airplane across the Atlantic Ocean. Read received many medals and later became a rear admiral in the navy.

The second flight took place a month later. The British team, with its captain John Alcock (1892–1919) and navigator Lieutenant Arthur Whitten Brown (1886–1948) flew a Vickers-Vimy converted bomber from Newfoundland across the Atlantic to Ireland on June 15–16, 1919. They covered 1,880 miles (3,026.8 kilometers) of open sea in 16 hours 12 minutes.

After that, it was a race to see who would be the first to fly nonstop between the United States and Europe. But no one seriously tried until 1926. In that year, René Fonck, a leading French ace of World War I, led a four-man crew attempting to fly from the United States to France. But his plane crashed shortly after takeoff. In May 1927 two other French war aces, Charles Nungesser and Francois Coli, took off from Paris, headed for New York, but their plane disappeared over the Atlantic Ocean. In the United States several well-known aviators, including Richard E. Byrd and Clarence Chamberlain, as well as Lindbergh, were preparing planes for the attempt.

In St. Louis, Lindbergh had convinced a group of local businessmen to finance him. The only condition they made was that he had to call his plane the *Spirit of St. Louis,* to which he readily agreed. After canvassing several manufacturers, he selected Ryan Airlines of San Diego, California, to build the plane for him, at a cost of $10,580. He flew to San Diego where he spent two months supervising its construction. His main worry was an adequate fuel supply, so the plane was equipped with five tanks, with a total capacity of 450 gallons (1,703.4 liters) of gasoline. To compensate for the added weight of the gasoline, Lindbergh decided to lighten the overall load by not taking a parachute, a radio, or even navigating instruments.

When the plane was finished, these were its specifications:

Wingspan: 46 feet (14 meters)
Length: 27 feet 8 inches (8.4 meters)
Height: 9 feet 10 inches (3 meters)

Engine: 9-cylinder Wright Whirlwind, 223 horsepower
Weight, loaded: 5,135 pounds (2,331.3 kilograms)
Air speed: 120 miles (193.2 kilometers) per hour

Satisfied with the plane's performance in test flights, Lindbergh took off for St. Louis and then New York, arriving on May 11. For the first time, he became the center of media attention, a new face in the race to cross the ocean, the only one who planned to fly alone. Some in the press called him "the Lone Eagle," while others dubbed him "the kid flyer" or "the flying fool."

On the morning of May 20, 1927, the *Spirit of St. Louis* stood poised at the end of the runway at Roosevelt Field, Long Island. At 7:51 a.m., Lindbergh tucked a paper bag containing five sandwiches and a canteen of water under his seat, buckled his seat belt, pulled goggles over his eyes, nodded to the mechanics below, and eased the throttle wide open. The heavily laden plane moved slowly forward, then picked up speed, and took off.

Lindbergh had carefully planned his route, marking charts for the entire trip in 100-mile (161-kilometer) segments, showing compass headings he would follow along a great circular route, the shortest distance between New York and Paris. As the plane soared along the coast of Long Island and New England, he kept careful notes of his direction, altitude, speed, and gasoline consumption in a log that he updated hourly. Flying at an altitude of 200 feet (61 meters), he soon reached Nova Scotia, then Newfoundland, and finally the Atlantic Ocean.

Flying through fog, ice, clouds, and occasional sunshine, Lindbergh methodically altered his course to conform to his preflight plan. His greatest enemy was drowsiness. He leaned out of his cockpit window to get fresh air, he slapped his face to keep awake, and he pulled out smelling salts from his first-aid kit to jolt him. Steadily, he flew onward until a speck of black on the water ahead drew his attention. He aimed the plane down toward the speck—a fishing boat.

He glided down to within 50 feet (15.2 meters) and yelled as loudly

THE *SPIRIT OF ST. LOUIS* OFFERS CHARLES LINDBERGH A BIRD'S-EYE VIEW OF THE EIFFEL TOWER AND THE SEINE RIVER BEYOND, SIGHTS HE COULD NOT TAKE IN DURING HIS INITIAL ARRIVAL IN PARIS, WHICH OCCURRED IN THE NIGHTTIME.

as he could, "Which way is Ireland?" But there was no answer. Lindbergh continued on his way eastward, confident that land could not be far away. It wasn't. In a short time, he spotted a rocky coast ahead— Ireland at last. He flew over the southwestern tip of England and the English Channel and, 33 hours after his departure from Roosevelt Field, flying at 4,000 feet (1,220 meters) at night, he reached the coast of France. Turning south, he flew toward the glow of the lights of Paris.

He circled the Eiffel Tower and searched for Le Bourget airport. Gradually descending, he landed safely at 10:24 p.m., Paris time. Looking out his cockpit window, he was stunned—outside was a mass of humanity, estimated at 150,000 people, who had come to the airport to see him land. His flight was front-page news all over the world. *The New York Times* used its biggest type to tell the story:

LINDBERGH DOES IT! TO PARIS IN 33½ HOURS;
FLIES 1,000 MILES THROUGH SNOW AND SLEET;
CHEERING FRENCH CARRY HIM OFF THE FIELD

As the news of the successful flight flashed around the world, President Calvin Coolidge sent the U.S.S. *Memphis* to take Lindbergh and the *Spirit of St. Louis* home, where he was cheered on the Mall in Washington, D.C., and at a ticker-tape parade in New York City. Honors piled up for Lindbergh—medals, degrees, parades, speeches, and the check for $25,000 from Orteig. He was promoted to the rank of colonel in the army air reserves, and the University of Wisconsin, from which he had dropped out, granted him the honorary degree of doctor of laws.

The shy, modest young aviator, only twenty-five years old, had become the most famous man in the world.

TRAGEDY STRIKES ON MAY 6, 1937, AS THE *HINDENBURG*'S ROUTINE LANDING ATTEMPT AT LAKEHURST, NEW JERSEY, RESULTS IN THE AIRSHIP EXPLODING INTO A BALL OF FLAMES. SOON AFTER, THE USE OF HYDROGEN AS A LIFTING AGENT WOULD BE PHASED OUT.

Other Notable Transatlantic Flights

Two weeks after Lindbergh's flight, on June 4, 1927, Clarence Chamberlain, with a passenger aboard, Charles A. Levine, flew in a Bellanca plane from New York to Germany, a nonstop flight of 3,911 miles (6,296.7 kilometers). As the second major transatlantic flight, it drew little attention in contrast to Lindbergh's.

Five years after Lindbergh's flight, in May 1932, Amelia Earhart, in a bright red Vega, flew nonstop from Newfoundland to Ireland, becoming the first woman to fly solo across the Atlantic. In 1937 she set off with a navigator to fly around the world, but disappeared over the Pacific Ocean. No trace of her has ever been found.

On May 6, 1937, the Hindenburg, a German zeppelin filled with hydrogen gas that gave it lift, was preparing to land in Lakehurst, New Jersey, after a transatlantic flight from Germany. It suddenly exploded, caught fire, and crashed. Of the ninety-seven people aboard, thirty-six died, and many survivors were horribly burned. The disaster marked the end of using hydrogen as a lifting agent. Today's lighter-than-air ships use helium, which does not burn.

In August 2003, an airplane made of balsa wood and Mylar, 6 feet (1.8 meters) long, weighing 11 pounds (5 kilograms), and filled with electronic navigational equipment, made the first nonstop crossing of the Atlantic by a model plane. Built by Maynard Hill of Silver Springs, Maryland, it flew 1,888 miles (3,039.7 kilometers) from Newfoundland to Ireland in 38 hours 23 minutes.

AN AIRMAIL PILOT AND HIS PLANE, ON A STOPOVER IN MINNESOTA IN 1925, ARE AN OBJECT OF FASCINATION FOR THIS GROUP OF BOYS. THE INVENTION OF THE AIRPLANE OPENED A NEW WORLD OF POSSIBILITY, OFFERING INCREASED ACCESS TO GOODS, SERVICES, AND ONCE-REMOTE PARTS OF THE GLOBE.

SIX

Highways in the Sky

Lindbergh's epic flight opened up a new era in aviation—no longer were the wide oceans a barrier to traveling quickly and easily between continents. He showed that airplanes could span the globe, making the world a smaller place. His remarkable flight inspired countless young people to learn to fly and many ambitious businessmen to organize commercial ventures to develop the growing field of aviation within the United States and abroad.

Even before Lindbergh, though, there had been some tentative moves toward passenger service. The first scheduled airline service in the United States started in Florida on January 1, 1914. The St. Petersburg–Tampa Air Boat Line, using a single-engined seaplane, carried one passenger on each of two trips per day across Tampa Bay (a distance of 18 miles [29 kilometers] in 23 minutes) for a fare of five dollars. The service lasted for one season before the airline folded. Further development of commercial airline service was interrupted by World War I, although it continued to grow when the war neared an end. But its primary purpose was not to convey passengers, but airmail.

On May 15, 1918, the U.S. Post Office Department inaugurated airmail service between Washington, D.C., and New York City. Flying Curtiss Jennies, Army Air Service pilots flew between the two cities, stopping in Philadelphia to refuel because of the planes' limited range. The trip from New York to Washington, a distance of 212 miles (341.2 kilometers), took 3 hours 20 minutes.

The Inverted Stamp

To mark the occasion of the first airmail service, the Post Office Department issued its first airmail stamp, a 24-cent red-and-blue stamp with a picture of the Curtiss Jenny. It became one of the most famous and valuable stamps in American history because one sheet of a hundred stamps was mistakenly printed with the Jenny upside down. In 1989 a plate block of four of the inverted Jenny stamps was sold at an auction in New York City. *The New York Times* headline the next day read, "$1 Million Stamp Sale Is Record for U.S. Issue."

As the Post Office Department expanded its airmail service after the war, it recruited former military pilots to fly surplus war planes. In those early days before weather reports, radio beacons, landing lights on airstrips, and navigational instruments, flying was a dangerous business. In 1920–1921, for example, nineteen airmail pilots were killed in crashes. As a result, in the mid-1920s, the government advertised for bids by private companies to carry airmail.

Among those who won a contract was Juan Trippe, a Yale graduate who gave up a job on Wall Street to start an air-taxi service for the vacationers between New York City and the beach resorts of Long Island. In 1927 he began airmail service between Key West, Florida, and Havana, Cuba, 80 miles (128.7 kilometers) away. It was the birth of Pan American World Airways, which grew to fly its famous "Clipper" planes to all parts of the world.

The importance of aviation to the national economy became clear to leaders in Washington. President Calvin Coolidge appointed a board, headed by Dwight Morrow, a prominent banker in New York, to recommend a national aviation policy. Morrow presented his report in 1926, concluding that, since aviation was vital to national defense, the federal government should support manufacturing companies. To give the public confidence in flying, he recommended that the government should set standards for planes and pilots and establish flyways—beacons on the ground to mark roads in the sky. Congress agreed and acted promptly, passing the Air Commerce Act of 1926.

The federal initiatives, which went into effect in 1927, plus Lindbergh's flight that same year, spurred the growth of aviation all the

NOW A STANDARD FEATURE ON MOST COMMERCIAL FLIGHTS, PASSENGERS ON THIS APRIL 26, 1925, TRIP ENJOY THE FIRST-EVER INFLIGHT MOVIE. EVEN IN ITS EARLIEST DAYS, THE INDUSTRY TOOK GREAT STRIDES TO ATTRACT PASSENGERS AND TO CATER TO THEIR NEEDS.

more. Within the next few years, many small local airlines began operations. From them, several major air carriers emerged: United, Transcontinental and Western (TWA), American, Eastern, and Pan American. But their planes were still relatively primitive, suitable for mail but unable to carry enough passengers to make a profit.

Although the public was beginning to accept air travel as a means of transportation, the aviation industry could not grow until it provided larger, safer, and more efficient airplanes. The next few years saw the emergence of new airplanes with powerful engines and navigational instruments as well as support systems of mechanics, airports, and managers.

The first commercial airplanes were small: Anthony Fokker produced a triengined plane that could carry eight passengers, while Henry Ford, better known as an automobile manufacturer, built a triengined plane called the Tin Goose that could carry twelve to fourteen passengers.

But it was not until 1933 that the first modern airliner went into service. The Boeing 247 was a twin-engined plane that cruised at 155 miles (249.6 kilometers) per hour, manufactured by the Boeing Aircraft Company of Seattle, Washington. It not only looked like a modern plane, but it provided some passenger comfort, which the earlier planes did not. The cabin walls were heavily insulated from engine noise, the seats were well upholstered, and an efficient ventilation system kept the air fresh. United Airlines bought sixty of the new planes and put them into service with a pilot, a copilot, and a new addition to the crew—stewardesses.

LIEUTENANT ELLEN CHURCH IS CREDITED WITH CONVINCING OFFI-CIALS THAT FLIGHTS SHOULD BE ACCOMPANIED BY TRAINED AND LI-CENSED NURSES. SHE IS ALSO CREDITED WITH BEING THE WORLD'S FIRST FLIGHT ATTENDANT. THIS PHOTOGRAPH IS FROM MARCH 1943, THOUGH SHE BEGAN SERVICE IN MAY 1930.

Stewardesses

The first flight attendants were all women, registered nurses called stewardesses. The first was Ellen Church, a nurse at French Hospital in San Francisco, who in 1930 suggested the idea to the airline, which agreed that the presence of young women on planes would be reassuring to passengers. It was, and is—but today these employees are called flight attendants—and are no longer required to be nurses or women. Of the more than 90,000 flight attendants working on commercial airlines in the United States today, 84 percent are female and 16 percent male.

To meet the competition, Transcontinental and Western Airlines turned to the Douglas Aircraft Company of Santa Monica, California. It designed a twin-engined plane called the DC-1 (Douglas Commercial Number One), which was too small and later expanded into the DC-2 and then into the DC-3. Introduced in 1936, the DC-3 carried twenty-one passengers. It revolutionized commercial air service because it was the first plane that made it possible for airlines to operate at a profit without transporting airmail as well.

The DC-3 was a technical departure in aircraft design; it was the first all-metal plane. Powered by two 1,000-horsepower engines, it came equipped with hydraulic landing gear, wing flaps, improved brakes, and many new cockpit and radio aids. Before long, all the airlines in the United States were buying DC-3s, and many foreign airlines just copied its design. By 1939, 75 percent of all American passengers were flying in DC-3s. During World War II, its military version, the C-47, was the backbone of wartime aviation, carrying supplies, paratroopers, and wounded men.

While the DC-3 was the workhorse plane of the airlines, more glamorous were the Pan American Clippers, powered by four engines, capable of landing on and taking off from water, and having large, comfortable interiors. The first was a Sikorsky S-40, used on routes from the United States to South America in 1931. Four years later, Pan American opened a stepping-stone route across 9,300 miles (14,973 kilometers) of the Pacific Ocean, from San Francisco to China, using Martin M-130 flying boats. Pan Am landed on islands that were to become famous in World War II— Hawaii, Midway, Wake, Guam, and the Philippines—before reaching Shanghai, China.

In 1939 Pan American began service between the United States and and England and also to Portugal with bigger and better Clippers built by Boeing. They were the biggest planes in service until the age of jumbo jets, equipped with the most powerful engines yet built, four 1,500-horsepower Wright Cyclones. Their interiors were luxurious,

SPECTATORS WATCH THE CHRISTENING BY PAN AMERICAN AIRWAYS OFFICIALS OF THE AMERICAN CLIPPER. IT BEGAN REGULAR SERVICE BETWEEN LOS ANGELES AND SAN FRANCISCO IN 1939.

License No. 1

Before 1927 pilots' licenses had been issued by the Aero Club of America, an affiliate of the Federation Aeronautique Internationale. On April 6, 1927, the Aeronautics Branch of the U.S. Department of Commerce, acting under the Air Commerce Act of 1926, began to issue them. Pilot's License Number 1 went to William P. McCracken, assistant secretary of commerce for aviation. On July 1, Mechanic's License Number 1 was issued to Frank Gates Gardner of Norfolk, Virginia.

with a bar, deluxe suites with comfortable lounge chairs, a dining room with tables, cabins with sleeping berths, and even flush toilets. The age of the Clippers ended with the development of giant four-engined planes that could travel long distances and land on the ground at airports near cities. Pan American World Airways, which was a leader in pioneering global routes, went out of business in 1991, the victim of financial pressures.

THIS WORLD WAR II SQUADRON OF P-51 MUSTANGS FLIES IN FORMATION OVER ENGLAND. FIGHTER PLANES BROUGHT THE BATTLES OF THE WAR TO A WHOLE NEW SPHERE—THE SKIES OF EUROPE AND BEYOND.

SEVEN

World War II

World War II started with airplane attacks in 1939 and ended with airplane attacks in 1945.

It started on September 1, 1939, when German Stukas dive-bombed Polish defenses in advance of an invading army, opening World War II in Europe.

In 1940, after a stunning defeat of France, Germany began an air assault on England in preparation for an invasion. After the air attack failed, Germany invaded the Soviet Union on June 22, 1941.

On December 7, 1941, Japanese planes launched from aircraft carriers made a sudden and surprise attack on Pearl Harbor in Hawaii, plunging the United States into the war.

It was over in August 1945. After four years of bitter fighting to conquer Japanese-held islands in the Pacific Ocean that could serve as airfields, American B 29s dropped two atomic bombs on Japan, ending the war.

In those six years between 1939 and 1945, World War II was fought on land, sea, underwater, and in the air all over the world. At first, the Allied powers—England, France, the Soviet Union, China, and the United States—suffered severe losses and casualties, but gradually the tide turned. The first sign that the Germans could be defeated came in the Battle of Britain, an air war that lasted from July to October 1940. Sending out hundreds of bombers each day, the German Luftwaffe pounded British airfields and factories, attempting to control the skies of Britain in advance of an invasion. But the British had two key defensive aids: radar, which told them where the Germans were, and Royal Air Force (RAF) pilots flying Hurricane and Spitfire fighters.

When the Germans made their first bombing raid on London, the British retaliated by an attack on Berlin. Enraged, the Nazis countered by launching massive bombing raids on London instead of trying to destroy the Royal Air Force. It proved to be a major strategic error. London suffered tremendous damage, but the RAF had time to recover and prevent the Germans from gaining air superiority over England. When the Germans called off the air war—and the invasion of England—it was a clear victory for the British. They had shot down 1,733 German aircraft while losing 915 of their own. Winston Churchill, the British prime minister, paid tribute to the young pilots of the RAF with these words: "Never in the field of human conflict was so much owed by so many to so few."

In the first years of the war in Europe, the United States became the "arsenal of democracy," supplying planes, ships, tanks, trucks, food, and munitions to England, almost isolated by German submarine warfare, and to the Soviet Union, reeling under Nazi attacks. When France fell to the Germans in June 1940, President Franklin D. Roosevelt called for Americans to produce 50,000 planes per year. To meet that goal, aircraft factories expanded rapidly, and auto manufacturers were temporarily converted to produce airplanes and tanks. By the end of the war, the United States had produced more than 300,000 military airplanes and built up an air force of more than two million men and women.

When the United States entered the war in 1941, it faced two enemies: the Germans in Europe and the Japanese in the Pacific. American military strategy called for fighting the Germans first, to prevent Europe from falling under Nazi domination, and the Japanese second. In practical terms, that meant supplying our British and Russian allies with arms and ammunition before American troops could arrive in Europe while, at the same time, trying to stop the Japanese from advancing further.

In early 1942 the Japanese seemed to be unstoppable. They had sunk or damaged eighteen American battleships and other warships at Pearl Harbor, captured the Philippine Islands, sunk two British battleships off Malaya, and invaded Indochina. The United States struck back in a bombing raid on Tokyo. In April 1942 Jimmy Doolittle led sixteen B-25s from an aircraft carrier, the *Hornet,* dropping bombs on Tokyo and other Japanese targets. The physical damage was minimal, but it brought the war home to the Japanese and raised morale for Americans, who had been shocked by the major defeats in the Pacific.

The turning point in the Pacific war came with the Battle of Midway, northwest of Hawaii, from June 4 to 7, 1942. The Japanese sent an armada

HERE 500-POUND (227-KILOGRAM) BOMBS DROPPED FROM A U.S. AIR FORCE FLYING FORTRESS TARGET AN OIL REFINERY, ON THE ITALIAN MAINLAND, FAR BELOW.

of two hundred ships—four aircraft carriers, seven battleships, and an invasion force of troopships—to capture Midway, destroy the American fleet, and open the way for further advances to Hawaii and Alaska. Unknown to the Japanese, the Americans had a crucial advantage: they had cracked the secret enemy naval codes and knew the Japanese plans in advance. Admiral Chester W. Nimitz stationed an American fleet of three aircraft carriers—the *Hornet,* the *Enterprise,* and the *Yorktown*—to block the Japanese.

At dawn on June 4, the major battle was carried out from a long distance—by airplanes launched from aircraft carriers 175 miles (281.6 kilometers) apart. After spotting the enemy carriers, American torpedo bombers attacked but failed to damage them, suffering heavy losses. Just as Japanese planes, rearmed and refueled, were preparing to take off, American dive-bombers attacked, destroying three Japanese carriers in minutes, and a fourth later. The enemy fleet turned back, its threat repelled.

Meanwhile, the tide was also turning in Europe. The Russians halted the German advance at Stalingrad, forcing a Nazi army to surrender. British and American armies invaded North Africa, then Sicily, and then mainland Italy while building up a powerful force in England for the invasion of France. Until then the war was brought to Germany on the wings of massive armadas of British Lancasters and American Flying Fortresses (B-17s) and Liberators (B-24s). Day and night, they bombed German airplane factories, oil supplies, ball-bearing plants, freight yards, bridges, and cities. Even though the damage was considerable, bombers did not win the war; it took soldiers on the ground to bring about victory.

When D-Day—the invasion of Europe—came on June 6, 1944, American, British, and Canadian troops landed on the shores of Normandy, France, under a cover of Allied planes, which were attacking German defenses and communications. The Allied planes had complete mastery of the air over France as tanks and men advanced toward Ger-

New weapons and aviation technologies resulted in a once-unthinkable level of mass destruction. Here, a Japanese boy cries amidst the rubble left by the explosion of the atomic bomb dropped on Hiroshima. About 80,000 people died instantly when the bomb was detonated on August 6, 1945.

The Debate

Ever since those fateful days in August 1945, the question has been debated: Was it necessary, or wise, to use the atomic bomb to force Japan to surrender? Opponents contend that such a dreadful weapon should never have been used, that a demonstration over less or nonpopulated areas would have been sufficient. Proponents reply that Japan would never have surrendered if the bomb had not been used. The alternative, an invasion, could have resulted in hundreds of thousands of American casualties, as shown in the determined Japanese defense of islands in the Pacific. Ask any veteran of World War II (as this writer is), and you will find an almost unanimous answer: Yes, it was necessary to use the bomb, and as a result, I am alive today.

many. Meanwhile, Russian troops on the eastern front blasted their way across Poland into Germany as well, crushing Nazi resistance and capturing Berlin. The Russian and Allied ground forces met at the River Elbe on April 25, 1945, and the Germans surrendered on May 7. The next day, May 8, was proclaimed V-E (Victory in Europe) Day.

After the Battle of Midway in the Pacific, American marines and soldiers methodically conquered Japanese-held islands on the sea road to Tokyo, establishing airfields from which to bomb Japan. Step by step, from Guadalcanal in the Solomon Islands to Truk in the Caroline Islands, and from Saipan and Iwo Jima to Okinawa south of Japan, Americans overcame bitter resistance and continued setting up airfields while suffering heavy losses themselves. Using new monster B-29 bombers, the air force battered Japan, causing massive firestorms in Tokyo and other Japanese cities.

The climax to the air war in Japan came on August 6, 1945, when the *Enola Gay*, a B-29 commanded by Lieutenant Colonel Paul Tibbets, dropped the first atomic bomb in history on the city of Hiroshima. The devastation was staggering: the city was leveled, tens of thousands of people were killed immediately, and by the end of the year 140,000 civilians were dead of burns and radiation poisoning. When the Japanese did not surrender immediately, another atomic bomb was dropped three days later on Nagasaki, destroying that city and killing 70,000 people. This time, Emperor Hirohito stepped in and convinced the

Japanese government that further resistance was futile. On August 15, 1945—V-J (Victory over Japan) Day—Japan surrendered, ending World War II.

As planes grew larger, so did their engines. This 25-foot (7.6-meter) CF6-6D turbo-fan jet engine was constructed for use in a Douglas DC-10 airliner.

The Jet Age

The modern era of the jet airplane began just before World War II started, when by an amazing coincidence two men unknown to one another, one in England and the other in Germany, invented jet-turbine engines. But it took years for the invention to become practical, first for military aircraft and then for commercial planes.

The Germans won the race to develop a jet-powered fighter plane in World War II, but by the time it entered service, it was too late to affect the outcome of the air war. Refining the design took years more, and it was not until the 1950s that jets began to replace piston engines in the world's civilian aircraft. Today almost all commercial—and military—airplanes are jet propelled.

What is a jet engine?

It is the product of applying Sir Isaac Newton's third law of motion: For every action there must be an equal and opposite reaction. If you burn a mixture of fuel and air in a chamber open at the rear and channel the force of the burning backward, then the chamber is propelled forward. If the chamber is within an airplane, the plane flies. But there is a problem—at higher altitudes there is not enough oxygen to keep the fire burning. To compensate for this, a turbine is added to force extra air into the burning chamber—a turbo supercharger.

The two young men who independently developed this system, Frank Whittle (1907–1996) in England and Hans von Ohain (1911–1998) in Germany, came up with a way to do just that in a jet engine.

Whittle, born in Coventry, England, enlisted in the Royal Air Force as soon as he could. As early as 1932, when he was a flight instructor in the RAF, he had an idea for a turbojet engine for which he eventually received a patent. But it took almost ten years, until May 15, 1941, in the third year of World War II, for his first jet airplane, the Gloster E 28, unofficially called the Pioneer, to fly. It initially traveled 200 yards (183 meters). Despite its apparent potential, the British dawdled in manufacturing jet fighters and never produced one during the war.

But the Germans did, based on the work of von Ohain. He conceived of a jet-turbine engine in 1933 while studying for his doctorate in physics at the University of Göttingen. After convincing the Heinkel Aircraft Company to allow him to work in its factory, he produced the Heinkel He 178, which some aviation historians call the first jet plane to actually fly—on August 27, 1939, five days before World War II broke out. Despite the pressures to produce the new weapon, it took several years to work out the bugs in the production of German jet fighters. It wasn't until late 1944 that the Messerschmitt 262, then the world's fastest airplane (at 541 miles [871 kilometers] per hour), entered combat.

It was apparent to military leaders everywhere that jets were the key to air superiority in the future. While commercial airlines stayed with bigger and better piston-driven airplanes, the U.S. Air Force and Navy—as well as several foreign countries—swiftly converted to jets, first for fighter planes and then for bombers.

But the post-war U.S. Air Force was a shadow of the mighty armada that had blanketed the world during the war. From a force of 2,253,000 men and women on V-J Day, air force enrollment dropped to 300,000 two years later, with fewer than 5,000 planes ready for combat. Rebuilding took time. A major step was taken in 1947, when the U.S. Air Force was formally established as its own branch of the military. Instead

Breaking the Sound Barrier

of being a division of the army, as it had been up to then, it was accorded the same status and recognition as the army and the navy. The air force began a careful long-range program of developing jet fighters, strategic bombers, and an intercontinental missile force capable of carrying atomic bombs over great distances.

Meanwhile, in the years after the end of World War II, commercial aviation in the United States and around the world began a remarkable period of growth, first with piston-propelled planes and later with jets. No longer burdened by wartime restrictions, airline operators looked for bigger, better, safer, and more comfortable planes to carry an increasing number of passengers now able to travel freely. In the late 1940s and early 1950s, traveling by air became an accepted mode of transportation not just for businesspeople in a hurry but for ordinary citizens on family visits or vacations. Flights between the United States and Europe became especially popular.

With the end of lucrative wartime construction contracts, the major manufacturers in the United States turned to commercial aircraft, churning out big, new piston-powered planes, mostly civilian versions of warplanes, capable of covering long distances. Lockheed produced its Constellation, which could fly at 280 miles (450.6 kilometers) per hour, reaching Paris in 13 hours. Douglas expanded its basic DC-3 into the DC-6, which crossed the continent in 10 hours. Boeing came up with the Stratocruiser, which made it to Paris in 12 hours. Even though many foreign airlines bought American-built planes, some na-

One of the major breakthroughs in the development of jet airplanes came on October 14, 1947, when Captain Charles "Chuck" Yeager, a fighter pilot in World War II, became the first person to fly faster than the speed of sound (1,088 feet [331.6 meters] per second or about 660 miles [1,062.6 kilometers] per hour). Flying in an experimental Bell XS-1 (named the *Glamorous Glennis* after his wife) at Muroc Air Base in California, he became the world's first supersonic pilot. Yeager reached the rank of brigadier general in the air force before he retired in 1975.

As it has always been, passenger comfort was a major focus of the commercial airline industry's attempt to appeal to the public. Sleeper seats were a new feature of the Comet 4, shown in a demonstration flight from 1958.

tions—particularly England, France, and the Soviet Union—developed their own models, too.

Different as they were, all these new planes had several things in common: four powerful new engines, propellers, noisy interiors, crowded seating, a capacity of about fifty to sixty passengers, high operating costs, and not altogether reliable schedules. They required long paved runways to land and take off from, which were provided in an accelerated program of airfield construction across the United States and abroad.

New airports in the United States could hardly keep up with the rising traffic. Arrival and departure statistics tell the story for the busiest airports:

> Hartsfield, Atlanta, Georgia, 76.9 million
> O'Hare, Chicago, Illinois, 66.6 million
> L.A. International, Los Angeles, California, 56.2 million
> Dallas-Fort Worth International, Texas, 52.8 million
> Sky Harbor, Phoenix, Arizona, 35.6 million
> Denver International, Colorado, 35.6 million

Overseas, the major airports were just as crowded. Their total arrivals and departures were:

> Heathrow, London, England, 63.3 million
> Haneda, Tokyo, Japan, 61.1 million
> Rhein-Main, Frankfurt, Germany, 48.5 million
> deGaulle, Paris, France, 48.3 million
> Schipol, Amsterdam, the Netherlands, 40.7 million

In the United States, the total number of passengers, in the latest year for which statistics are available, reached 640 million, according to the Federal Aviation Administration (FAA), and has remained at similar levels since. Worldwide, one industry estimate is that all airlines, both American and foreign, now carry about two billion passengers per year.

As airlines and passenger traffic grew, so did the infrastructure necessary to support them—large numbers of mechanics, flight attendants, reservation clerks, travel agents, food suppliers, airport-maintenance crews, baggage handlers, as well as the pilots and copilots, air-traffic controllers, and weather forecasters needed for flight operations.

With the growth of air traffic, the airlines responded with jets that could fly longer distances at greater speeds, which were cheaper to operate than piston-driven airplanes and so more profitable for the airlines. The first commercial jet airliner, a British De Havilland Comet, began service in 1952, carrying forty-four passengers at 450 miles (724.2 kilometers) per hour to Johannesburg, South Africa. Three years later, in 1955, the Soviet Union introduced its first jet airliner, the Tupolev-104, which carried 100 passengers.

The Americans were not far behind. In 1957 Boeing produced the 707, with room for 143 passengers. It flew at a speed close to 600 miles (966 kilometers) per hour, powered by giant new Pratt & Whitney engines. A year later, Douglas Aircraft introduced its new DC-8s, which performed about as well.

In the United States, three major companies—Boeing, Douglas, and Lockheed—competed for the expanding jet-travel market. In 1969 Boeing introduced the wide-bodied jumbo four-engined 747, as tall as a five-story building and 231 feet (70.4 meters) long with a wingspan of 195 feet (59.4 meters). It carried up to 452 passengers at a speed of more than 500 miles (805 kilometers) per hour. Douglas produced its DC-10, slightly smaller, seating about 250 passengers, with three engines, two under the wings and one on the tail. Lockheed also came up with a wide-bodied plane, the L-1011, which also had three engines and had a seating capacity of three hundred. It was no wonder that the Boeing 747 became the world's most successful jetliner—and still is.

With success, however, came problems—passenger dissatisfaction with jammed seating, unappealing food, crowded highways leading to airports, long walks at the airports, long waits at check-in desks, lost

FIVE DC-8'S ARE DOCKED, WAITING TO RECEIVE TRAVELERS, AT THIS CONCOURSE PROJECTING FROM THE UNITED AIRLINES PASSENGER TERMINAL AT SAN FRANCISCO INTERNATIONAL AIRPORT. THE 1960S SAW A SURGE IN THE POPULARITY OF AIR TRAVEL.

The Fastest Plane

Lockheed built the world's fastest airplane, the air force's SR-71 Blackbird high-altitude reconnaissance jet, which flew at more than three times the speed of sound. On its final flight, it flew from Los Angeles to Washington, D.C., in 1 hour 4 minutes 19 seconds, with an average speed of 2,144 miles (3,450.4 kilometers) per hour. Some sources credit another plane with being the fastest—North American's X-15, which flew in 1967 at 4,534 miles (7,297 kilometers) per hour, six times the speed of sound, but it was only an experimental model.

baggage, and a complicated fare structure. Even though the airlines advertised low-cost coach fares, they were not always available, especially for business travelers who frequently had to make their reservations at the last minute.

Flying became even more complex after terrorists hijacked passenger planes and flew them into the World Trade Center in New York City and damaged the Pentagon in Washington, D.C., on September 11, 2001. After stringent security search measures were imposed, most Americans accepted the necessity of such checks, but it meant more delays and waiting at airports.

Despite the new travel climate, passenger traffic boomed but, ironically, profits for the airline industry—both manufacturers and airlines—sagged because of high operating costs and cut-throat competition. The result was bankruptcies and mergers. By 2003 there were only seven major airlines operating in the United States, listed here in order of the number of passengers carried—Delta, Southwest, American, United, Northwest, U.S. Airways, and Continental—but also dozens of smaller and regional airlines. Gone were familiar names such as Pan American, Eastern, Braniff, and TWA.

A similar series of mergers took place among manufacturers. After Douglas and McDonnell joined forces, the Douglas DC-10 became the MD (McDonnell Douglas) II. Seven years later another merger took place: Boeing took over the McDonnell-Douglas Corporation and the combination became the Boeing Company, the largest commercial aircraft-manufacturing company in the United States. Another merged company, Lockheed-Martin, became the largest contractor for the U.S. Department of Defense, producing warplanes.

Glamour and innovation have historically been two elements airlines hyped in marketing commercial flights to the public. Before flying became more commonplace, many air customers were seduced by the mystique and alluring image air travel seemed to project. Here, models have locked hands to show off the new, roomier interior of this passenger plane about to be completed.

Although foreign countries bought many American-built planes, they also developed their own aviation industries, manufacturing planes and promoting their own airlines. Americans became familiar with—and traveled on—planes operated by British Airways, Lufthansa (Germany), Air France, Finn Air, Alitalia, El Al (Israel), Icelandic, Japan Airways, Qantas (Australia), and many others. Most of them, but not all, used American-made planes, particularly the Boeing 747.

But few Americans were familiar with Aeroflot, the Soviet state-controlled airline, which at one time was the largest airline in the world. Before the Soviet Union broke up in 1991, Aeroflot owned a fleet of 11,000 airplanes and helicopters, employing 20,000 pilots to cover 620,000 miles (997,793 kilometers) of domestic routes. When the Soviet Union disbanded, Aeroflot was broken up into regional airlines, the biggest one in Russia—the largest of the former Soviet republics. Today the Aeroflot-Russian Airline flies to 150 cities around the world, mostly in Russian-built planes, but with a few made by Aerobus and Boeing.

Not content to see the United States dominate commercial sales, a French company named Sud Aviation organized a Europe-wide group, Airbus Industrie, to compete in the world market, including the United States. During the 1970s, it began to manufacture wide-bodied twin-engined planes for the short-haul market, and later it produced bigger planes to match the Boeing 747s. Soon Airbus was a major airplane manufacturer competing with Boeing in supplying the world's airlines and in 2003 actually surpassing Boeing in commercial aircraft sales.

Boeing bowed out of the race to build the world's first supersonic commercial jet plane because of the high costs involved. That technical achievement was left to two competitors: the Soviet Union and a combination of two European companies, British Aerospace and

General Aviation

Aerospatiale, with generous subsidies from the British and French governments. A Soviet plane, the Tupolev TU-144, was the first to get off the ground in supersonic test flights in 1968, but the British-French offering was not far behind. It took several years, though, before supersonic jets were ready for commercial service—and they proved to be economically unviable.

The British-French plane, the Concorde, was a marvel of engineering, with a long pointed nose, somewhat like an anteater; a wide rear delta-shaped wing; and a narrow body, only 9 feet 6 inches (2.7 meters) wide, which could seat a hundred passengers. Its four powerful engines developed a speed of 1,336 miles (2,150 kilometers) per hour, twice the speed of sound, which meant that it could cross the Atlantic Ocean in a little more than three hours, just about half the time it took a Boeing 747.

Only two airlines, British Airways and Air France, flew Concordes when they made their debut in January 1976 with flights from London to Bahrain in the Persian Gulf and from Paris to Rio de Janeiro. Despite its speed, the Concorde had several flaws. Most important, it created a loud sonic boom, which led to a ban on supersonic flight over land, making flying time longer than it would have been otherwise. It was costly, too. The price for a one-way passage from London to New York, for example, was nearly $6,000, ten times the prevailing fare, which

In addition to military and commercial aviation, a third category is called general, a term used to describe flying in small planes by individuals for pleasure, by companies for executive travel, by crop dusters, and by flight instructors. Although general aviation has not grown to vast proportions, as some early optimists estimated, it has reached impressive numbers. For example, the United States has about 250,000 licensed private pilots (more than the 140,000 licensed airline pilots) and about 214,000 licensed private airplanes, mostly small single-engined piston-driven planes but including some twin-engined jets capable of carrying ten passengers (compared to about 9,000 commercial aircraft). In addition, there are 18,000 public use airports and landing strips (compared to about 600 with control towers for commercial use).

The fact that the Concorde was sleek, powerful, and above all, fast accounted for its successful run. It was pulled from operation in 2003.

meant that only movie stars, celebrities, and top business executives used it. And, despite its luxurious aura, it was crowded and uncomfortable inside because of its narrow fuselage.

A beautiful plane that drew public admiration wherever it flew, it had many critics, mainly because of the sonic boom. It was also expensive to fly, requiring four times as much fuel per passenger as a 747 to cross the Atlantic. When business travel dropped because of an economic recession in the early 2000s, Air France and British Airways decided that they could no longer operate Concordes. The famed aircraft made their last flights in October 2003, ending twenty-seven years of supersonic air travel. In their wake, they left behind several Concordes in air museums around the world and a big question: will supersonic air travel be possible again in the future?

AIRPLANE TECHNOLOGY LED TO RAPID ADVANCES IN SPACE EXPLORATION THAT MARKED THE LATTER DECADES OF THE TWENTIETH CENTURY AND BEYOND. HERE, THE SPACE SHUTTLE *ATLANTIS* LIFTS OFF FROM FLORIDA'S KENNEDY SPACE CENTER ON SEPTEMBER 8, 2000, ON A MISSION TO SUPPLY THE *INTERNATIONAL SPACE STATION*.

Man on the Moon

Future generations may look back at our time and remember it because we took our first tentative steps to explore outer space and the stars. If they do, they will probably mark the birth of the modern space age on March 16, 1926, when Robert Goddard (1882–1945) tested a liquid-fueled rocket on his aunt's farm outside Worcester, Massachusetts. It climbed 41 feet (12.5 meters) in 1.4 seconds and traveled a distance of 184 feet (56.1 meters)—the first successful flight in the history of modern rocketry.

But it was in another country, Germany, a wartime enemy of the United States, that his ideas were put to work. Nazi Germany fired rockets with extraordinary destructive power to bomb England mercilessly near the end of World War II. When Germany was defeated, American experts entered Pennemunde, the German rocket-development center, and began asking engineers a slew of technical questions.

"Why don't you ask your own Dr. Goddard?" the Germans replied. They knew, even if the Americans did not, that Goddard was "the father of modern rocketry." The American military whisked many of the German experts, led by Wernher von Braun, to the United States to work on American rocket and missile programs.

From then on, the United States and the Soviet Union, although they had been allies in World War II, faced off in the "Cold War," each thinking the other was a threat. Those fears led to a double-barreled race to develop new and more powerful rockets to explore space and for intercontinental ballistic missiles (ICBMs) to carry atomic bombs. Both countries developed arsenals of weapons of mass destruction, but the threat of nuclear war receded in 1991 with the disintegration of the Soviet Union into several independent nations.

The desire to build more powerful rockets also led to the exploration of space, with both countries working independently at first and later in cooperation. Americans were stunned when the Soviet Union took the lead by launching the first satellite to orbit the earth in 1957 and then the first man into space in 1961. After that shock, the United States poured money and resources into a massive space program and achieved a historic success by landing men on the moon in 1969.

APOLLO 11 ASTRONAUT EDWIN E. "BUZZ" ALDRIN JR., THE SECOND PERSON TO SET FOOT ON THE MOON, WALKS NEAR ONE OF THE LEGS OF THE LANDING MODULE THE EAGLE DURING THE HISTORIC JULY 1969 MISSION.

Here is a time line of milestones in space exploration:

1957 The Soviet Union launches *Sputnik,* the first artificial satellite.

1958 The United States launches its first satellite, *Explorer 1.*
The National Aeronautics and Space Administration (NASA) is created.

1961 A Russian, Yuri Gagarin, becomes the first person to orbit the earth.
Alan Shepard becomes the first American to be sent into space; he travels 115 miles (185.1 kilometers) in 15 minutes.
President Kennedy announces that the United States will put a man on the moon in a decade.

1962 John Glenn becomes the first U.S. astronaut to orbit the earth.

1963 Valentina Tereshkova, a Russian, becomes the first woman to be sent into space.

1964 The United States launches *Mariner 4* to Mars, which transmits pictures back to the earth.

1965 Soviet cosmonaut Major Alexei Leonov becomes the first man to leave his ship and "walk" in space.
Major Edward H. White becomes the first American astronaut to "walk" in space.

1968 Three Americans—Colonel Frank Borman, Captain James Lovell, and Major William Anders—fly around the moon.

1969 Americans Neil Armstrong and Edwin Aldrin land on the moon, at 4:17 p.m. EDT on July 20; Armstrong steps down first, followed by Aldrin.

1971 The Soviet Union launches the first space station, *Salyut.*

1973 The United States launches its first space station, *Skylab.*

1978 The American probes *Venus 1* and *Venus 2* land on the planet for which they are named.

1979 *Pioneer 11* flies by Saturn.
Skylab is abandoned, falls from its orbit, and disintegrates.

1981 The U.S. space shuttle *Columbia* makes its first flight.

1983 Sally Ride becomes the first American woman to be sent into space.

1986 The space shuttle *Challenger* explodes after launch, killing all aboard.
The Soviet Union launches its first space station, *Mir.*

1990 The United States sends the Hubble space telescope into orbit.

1997 The U.S. *Pathfinder* lands on Mars, recording and transmitting pictures.

1998 Work begins on an international space station.

2000 The first crew of Russian and American astronauts reaches the space station.

2001 Soviets abandon *Mir,* which burns up as it falls to Earth.

2003 The American space shuttle *Columbia* explodes as it descends for a landing, killing all astronauts aboard.
China sends its first astronaut into space, becoming the third nation with a manned space program.

2004 President George W. Bush announces a new program to construct a permanent moon station and send an astronaut to Mars.
U.S. robots *Spirit* and *Opportunity* land on Mars, recording and sending back pictures.
U.S. space probe *Cassini* reaches Saturn and sends back images of its rings.

2005 The European spacecraft *Huygens* arrives at Saturn's moon Titan, the first human-made voyager to land on another planet's moon.

The *Columbia* disaster delayed the U.S. space program, which continued at a slow pace. An investigation laid the blame on a hole in a wing caused by a falling tile moments after launch, which resulted in the disintegration of the shuttle as it approached the earth for a landing.

Despite that loss, NASA remained committed to an ambitious space program. One of its top priorities will be to complete the international space station, which will be about twice the size of a football field, floating 220 miles (354.1 kilometers) above the earth's surface. It will serve as a center of research about various forms of life in space and, perhaps, as a launching pad for voyages farther into the unknown.

At the same time, NASA is continuing to send its unmanned probes into space, not only to nearby planets such as Mars but to far-distant ones at the outer reaches of the universe. For example, in the year 2003, *Voyager 1,* after traveling more than 8 billion miles from Earth in twenty-six years, reached the far frontier of the solar system—and is still going. From it and its sister ship, *Voyager 2,* NASA scientists hope to receive radio signals that will tell us more about the origins and content of the universe.

Beyond that, NASA's scientists and engineers have embarked on a long-range program to set up a permanent manned station on the moon and after that to send a manned mission to Mars.

Helicopters

Igor Sikorsky (1889–1972) did not invent the helicopter, but he designed and built the first practical one. The idea of a machine that can rise and descend vertically is centuries old, dating back to a sketch by Leonardo da Vinci in about 1500. But it took a long time to build one that worked. The first modern helicopter large enough to carry a pilot was built by Paul Cornu in France in

THE VS-300, CREATED BY IGOR SIKORSKY, BECAME THE FIRST SUCCESSFUL HELICOPTER. IN 1941 IT ESTABLISHED A WORLD RECORD FLIGHT OF 1 HOUR 32 MINUTES 26 SECONDS.

1907, but it rose for only a few seconds. In 1936 Heinrich Focke in Germany built one with twin overhead rotors that flew briefly but never became popular.

The modern helicopter that we know today is largely a legacy of Sikorsky, who was an aeronautical pioneer in Russia before he immigrated to the United States after the Russian Revolution of 1917. In the United States, he organized the Sikorsky Aero Engineering Corporation to manufacture airplanes. In 1939 he built a single-rotor helicopter, the VS-300, for the U.S. Army, the prototype of the modern "choppers" used by the military, police, television stations, rescue missions in remote areas, and medical-emergency crews.

Although they seem to be everywhere on television news, the number of helicopters in use is relatively small. The latest findings, according to AFaF, indicate that about 7,100 helicopters are used by civilian agencies in the United States and 7,131 by the military.

SR-71 BLACKBIRDS WERE DEVELOPED MORE THAN THIRTY YEARS AGO. THEY CAN FLY MORE THAN 2,200 MILES (3,541 KILOMETERS) PER HOUR, OR MORE THAN THREE TIMES THE SPEED OF SOUND, AT ALTITUDES OF MORE THAN 85,000 FEET (26 KILOMETERS).

The Future

One of the favorite jokes in the aviation industry is that the crew of airliners in the future will consist of a pilot and a dog. The pilot will sit in the cockpit watching a bank of computers, while the dog will be trained to bite the pilot if he or she tries to fly the airplane.

The joke is a reference to the potential growth of unmanned aerial vehicles (UAVs)— planes without pilots flown by computerized programs. The military is already using UAVs for reconnaissance purposes and soon, perhaps as early as 2020, will use them for combat, particularly bombing missions. Although many of today's commercial flights are directed by computers and electronics, it seems unlikely that the public will accept flying in unmanned passenger airplanes. The presence of a seasoned pilot at the controls is reassuring to most people and essential in an emergency—after all, computers are known to malfunction occasionally. But pilotless airplanes seem likely in the not-too-distant future for flights that carry overnight packages, perform geological surveys, fight forest fires, and even patrol borders.

In the more than one hundred years since the invention of the airplane, advances in aviation have been spectacular. A great industry was born, offering relatively cheap transportation to millions of men and women around the world, opening up foreign countries to travel, providing jobs for many, boosting national economies, and promoting advanced technology and scientific discoveries. Along with the benefits, there have been some negative aspects as well; for example, in wartime, airplanes and missiles have made it possible to deliver bigger and more deadly bombs, including atomic weapons, faster and more efficiently.

What will happen in the next one hundred years?

We don't know, of course, but it seems unlikely that the pace of building bigger and faster airplanes will continue. Most aviation historians think that the industry has matured and that any further improvements will be modest. Some observers confine their hopes to quicker transportation from city centers to airports, more efficient boarding and disembarking procedures, a more flexible fare structure, faster and more efficient flights, more comfortable interiors, the development of alternative fuels such as hydrogen for the day when fossil fuels like gasoline disappear, and, above all, the elimination of terrorist threats.

With the demise of the Concorde in 2003, visions of supersonic travel accessible to the general public have faded, at least for the near future. The world's two biggest manufacturers, Boeing and Airbus, are pursuing different approaches to profitability by building new planes with more modest goals and trading speed for efficiency. Boeing's newest plane, the 7E7 (the E standing for Efficiency), built with new lightweight composite materials, will require about 20 percent less fuel, with a range of 8,000 miles (12,875 kilometers) nonstop. It can carry between 200 and 250 passengers, fewer than Boeing's 747. Airbus, on the other hand, is building a giant double-decker jet, the A-380, that will carry 555 passengers at first and eventually perhaps as many as 800, which will make it the largest plane in commercial service when it begins operations.

Some visionaries, noting the remarkable achievements in the first hundred years of flight, foresee equally great advances ahead both on Earth and in space in the next hundred years.

Here on Earth, they see large planes flying at hypersonic speeds three, four, and even ten times the speed of sound, to distant destinations; more small planes making easy, short trips; even air-taxi helicopters taking people from their homes to airports or other destinations;

THE ANSARI X PRIZE WAS CLAIMED ON OCTOBER 4, 2004, BY SPACESHIPONE. THE $10-MIL-LION PURSE WAS TO BE AWARDED TO THE FIRST TEAM TO SEND A PILOTED CRAFT UP TO A 100-KILOMETER (62.5-MILE) ALTITUDE TWICE IN ONE WEEK. THE CRAFT ALSO HAD TO BE CARRYING ABOUT 400 POUNDS (180 KILOGRAMS) OF EXTRA BAGGAGE, ENOUGH TO REPRESENT THE WEIGHT OF TWO ADDITIONAL PASSENGERS. AT ITS HIGHEST POINT, THE ROCKET PLANE ACHIEVED AN ALTI-TUDE OF 69.6 MILES (112 KILOMETERS). "IT IS A THRILL THAT I THINK EVERYBODY SHOULD HAVE ONCE IN A LIFETIME," SAID ASTRONAUT BRIAN BINNIE OF HIS FEAT.

the development of new fuel sources to replace petroleum products; and, above all, a peaceful world in which the threat of airplanes and missiles carrying atomic weapons will be eliminated.

Looking at the stars, NASA scientists and engineers are already planning to establish a permanent manned station on the moon, sending an astronaut to Mars, and continuing a program of dispatching unmanned photographic probes toward distant stars and planets. Although the science-fiction fantasy of average citizens traveling to the moon, Mars, and outer space is remote, all those voyages are possible for intrepid astronauts and explorers, perhaps within your lifetime. Undaunted by the scientific and financial difficulties, many observers see the exploration of space by earthbound men and women as the next major challenge of aviation.

What do you think?

aileron—The movable extension of an aircraft's wings used to raise one wing and lower the other during a turn.

aviation—The operation of heavier-than-air flying machines.

elevator—A movable surface on an aircraft's wings that permits it to go up or down under a pilot's control.

fuselage—The body of an aircraft.

glider—A heavier-than-air craft without any engine or power.

helicopter—A flying machine that can go directly up or down.

horsepower—A unit of energy equivalent to 743.7 watts or 33,000 pounds (14,968.5 kilograms) per minute.

internal-combustion engine—An enclosed device that uses the explosive power of burning fuel and air to push a piston that then turns a crankshaft.

lift—The upward force created by air moving over and under the wings of an aircraft.

propeller—Several blades, usually two, that rotate on a shaft driven by an engine that pulls an airplane through the air.

rudder—A control, usually at the rear of an aircraft, that can be moved to make horizontal right or left turns.

turbine—An engine with several blades in which the energy of a moving gas is converted into mechanical motion by spinning the blades.

zeppelin—A rigid lighter-than-air flying machine named after Count Ferdinand von Zeppelin.

1500?
Leonardo da Vinci creates sketches of a flying machine.

1783
The Montgolfier brothers, Étienne and Joseph, demonstrate the first balloon flights in France.

1804
In England, Sir George Cayley experiments and writes about the shape of wings in gliders.

1890
In France, Clement Ader uses a steam engine to lift a plane a few inches off the ground.

1891
Otto Lilienthal, studying the flight of birds in Germany, begins glider experiments.

1892
Samuel P. Langley experiments in Washington, D.C., with model steam-powered flying machines.

1894
In England, Sir Hiram Maxim builds a model flying machine powered by a steam engine that rises but crashes.
Octave Chanute writes *Progress in Flying Machines* and begins glider experiments near Chicago.

1900
The first rigid-frame airship flight is made by Count Ferdinand von Zeppelin of Germany.

1903
Samuel Langley builds a huge gasoline-powered flying machine that crashes during testing.

Orville and Wilbur Wright make the first successful manned flights using a gasoline engine at Kitty Hawk, North Carolina.

1907
A Frenchman, Paul Cornu, builds the first helicopter, which lifts several inches off the ground.

1909
Glenn Curtiss opens the first U.S. airplane-manufacturing company.
The first international air show is held in Rheims, France.
The U.S. Army buys its first airplane from the Wright brothers.
Frenchman Louis Bleriot becomes the first person to fly across the English Channel.

1911
Glenn Curtiss is granted a patent for a seaplane equipped with pontoons to land and take off in water.

1913
Russian Igor Sikorsky designs and flies the first four-engined plane.

1914
The first scheduled airline flights begin between St. Petersburg and Tampa, Florida.

1915
German dirigibles bomb England in World War I.

1918
Airmail service begins between Washington, D.C., and New York City. The first airmail stamp is issued.

1919
Lieutenant Commander Albert Read and his crew of five make, in stages, the first Atlantic crossing by air.
Captain John Alcock and Lieutenant Arthur Whitten Brown make the first non-stop Atlantic crossing, from Canada to Ireland.

1921
Bombs dropped from an airplane sink a battleship for the first time.

1922
The U.S.S. *Langley,* the first American aircraft carrier, is commissioned.

1926
Lieutenant Commander Richard E. Byrd makes the first flight over the North Pole.

1927

Charles Lindbergh makes the first solo, nonstop crossing of the Atlantic, flying from New York to Paris.

1928

The *Graf Zeppelin* makes the first Atlantic crossing with paying passengers.

1929

Richard E. Byrd makes the first flight over the South Pole.

1930

Ellen Church, a registered nurse, becomes the first stewardess, working a flight between San Francisco and Cheyenne.

1930

Frank Whittle of the British Royal Air Force invents a turbojet engine.

1932

Amelia Earhart becomes the first woman to fly solo across the Atlantic.

1933

Wiley Post becomes the first person to fly solo around the world.
United Airlines begins passenger service with a Boeing 247.

1935

Hans von Ohain of Germany invents a jet engine.
The China Clipper begins the first transpacific passenger service.
Douglas Aircraft Company builds its first DC-3.

1937

Amelia Earhart disappears in a flight over the Pacific Ocean.
The *Hindenburg* explodes and burns at Lakehurst, New Jersey.

1940

In the Battle of Britain, the Royal Air Force halts attacks by the German Luftwaffe.

1941

Japanese planes, launched from aircraft carriers, bomb Pearl Harbor, plunging the United States into war.

1942

American planes, launched from an aircraft carrier, drop bombs on Tokyo.

1943

U.S. Air Force B-17s make the first bombing raid on Germany.

1944
The first jet fighters, German Me 262s, are sent into battle.

1945
Air Force B-29s drop atomic bombs on the Japanese cities of Hiroshima and Nagasaki.

1947
The U.S. Air Force is designated as an organization parallel to the army and navy. Captain Charles E. Yeager makes the first supersonic flight.

1948
The United States initiates the Berlin airlift to break a Soviet blockade.

1952
The first commercial jet airliner, Britain's De Havilland Comet, flies from London to Johannesburg, South Africa.

1955
The first class of cadets enters the new Air Force Academy in Colorado.

1957
The first U.S. jet transport, the Boeing 707, enters service.

1960
A U.S. U-2 spy plane is shot down over the Soviet Union.

1970
The first jumbo-jet airliner, the Boeing 747, enters service.

1976
The first supersonic jet airliner, the Concorde, begins flights.

1986
Dick Rutan and Jeana Yeager make the first nonstop flight around the world without refueling, in the lightweight *Voyager*.

1988
Libyan terrorists bring down a Pan Am 747 at Lockerbie, Scotland, resulting in 270 casualties.

1996
A Trans World Airlines 747 explodes and crashes into the ocean off Long Island, resulting in 230 casualties.

1999
Bertrand Piccard and Brian Jones make the first nonstop around-the-world balloon trip in their Breitling Orbiter 3.

2001
Terrorists hijack four airliners, crash two into New York's World Trade Center, and one into the Pentagon in Washington, D.C. A fourth crashes in Pennsylvania with all aboard killed.

2003
The Concorde is pulled out of service.

Pioneers in Aviation

Alcock and Brown—Captain John Alcock (1892–1919) and Lieutenant Arthur Whitten Brown (1886–1948) of England made the first nonstop transatlantic flight in 1919.

Bleriot, Louis (1872–1936)—French aviator; the first person to fly across the English Channel in an airplane, in 1909.

Byrd, Richard E. (1888–1957)—American naval officer; he and Floyd Bennett were the first to fly over the North Pole (1926) and, with Bernt Balchen, the South Pole (1929).

Cayley, Sir George (1773–1857)—English scientist who experimented with gliders, wing surfaces, rudders, and elevators.

Chanute, Octave (1832–1910)—American engineer; he experimented with and wrote about the wing surfaces of gliders.

Cornu, Paul (1881–1944)—French experimenter; built a primitive helicopter that lifted 5 feet (1.5 meters) above the ground for 20 seconds.

Curtiss, Glenn (1878–1930)—Pilot and designer; in 1911 he applied for a patent for a seaplane equipped with pontoons to land on water, also organized the Curtiss Airplane Company.

Earhart, Amelia (1898–1937)—First woman to cross the Atlantic by airplane (1928), first to make solo transatlantic flight (1932), first to fly solo from Honolulu to California (1935), disappeared during a transpacific flight (1937).

Fokker, Anthony (1890–1939)—Dutch airplane designer of planes for Germany in World War I and of American planes after the war.

Garros, Roland (1888–1918)—French flier; first to fly across the Mediterranean Sea, in 1913; in World War I, devised machine gun to fire between turns of a propeller in a fighter plane.

Langley, Samuel P. (1834–1906)—American scientist; secretary of the Smithsonian Institution, designed a steam-powered aircraft that failed to fly.

Leonardo da Vinci (1452–1519)—Italian painter, sculptor, architect, engineer; drew first sketches of a flying machine.

Lilienthal, Otto (1848–1906)—German aeronautical engineer; designed and flew in gliders, starting in 1891.

Lindbergh, Charles A. (1902–1974)—American aviator; made the first solo transatlantic flight, from New York to Paris, in 1927.

Montgolfier, Joseph (1740–1810) and Étienne (1745–1799)—French inventors of the first practical hot-air balloon in 1783; made several test flights over Paris.

Ohain, Hans von (1911–1998)—German physicist; invented a jet engine in 1935 which powered an experimental plane in 1939, in this way becoming the first jet airplane.

Post, Wiley (1899–1935)—American aviator; made solo flight around the world in 1933 in 7 days 19 hours.

Read, Arthur Cushing (1887–1967)—American naval officer; made the first transatlantic flight, with several stops, in 1919, from Newfoundland via the Azores to Portugal.

Richthofen, Manfred von (1892–1918)—German fighter pilot; known as the "Red Baron," a leading ace in World War I credited with shooting down about eighty Allied planes.

Santos-Dumont, Alberto (1873–1932)—Brazilian experimenter; flew in a powered balloon in 1898, also made short powered aircraft flights in 1906.

Sikorsky, Igor (1889–1972)—Russian-born airplane designer; became an American citizen in 1928, perfected a practical helicopter in 1939.

Smith, Frederick W. (1944–)—American entrepreneur; started overnight package delivery system by air in 1973.

Tupolev, Andrey (1888–1972)—Russian-born designer and manufacturer of many planes, including jet airliners and supersonic planes.

Whittle, Frank (1907–1996)—British aeronautical engineer in the Royal Air Force; in 1930 invented a turbojet engine.

Wright, Wilbur (1867–1912) and Orville (1871–1948)—Brothers from Dayton, Ohio; made the first controlled powered aircraft flight in 1903.

Yeager, Charles (1923–)—American air force test pilot; first to fly faster than the speed of sound, in 1947.

Zeppelin, Count Ferdinand von (1838–1917)—German designer; built the first motor-driven rigid dirigible, named after him, in 1900.

http://www.aviation-history.com/
Contains photographs and information on the faces, names, and particular aircraft that have left a mark on the history of aviation.

http://www.first-to-fly.com/
A virtual aviation museum, with particular focus on the contributions of the Wright brothers.

http://www.wpafb.af.mil/museum/
The Web site of the United States Air Force Museum. Offers a detailed look at this branch of the military and contains a special feature for repeat visitors, Aircraft of the Week.

http://inventors.about.com/library/inventors/blairplane.htm
A general overview of aviation history, with links to various articles covering history, technology, and innovations.

http://www.thespaceplace.com/history/rocket2.html
A site that specifically examines aviation, rocketry, and the pioneers of space exploration.

http://www.century-of-flight.freeola.com/
This site offers a historical overview, celebrating the first century of flight.

http://airlines.afriqonline.com/features/usa.htm
Offers a history of commercial aviation and the development of the airline industry.

Bibliography

Berg, A. Scott. *Lindbergh.* New York: Putnam, 1998.

Boyne, Walter J. *Beyond the Wild Blue: A History of the U.S. Air Force, 1947–1997.* New York: St. Martin's, 1997.

———. *The Smithsonian Book of Flight.* Avenel, NJ: Wings Books, 1987.

*Brown, Travis. *Historic First Patents.* Metuchen, NJ: Scarecrow Press, 1994.

Crouch, Tom. *The Bishop's Boys: A Life of Wilbur and Orville Wright.* New York: Norton, 1989.

Davidson, Janet F., and Michael S. Sweeney. *On the Move: Transportation and the American Story.* Washington, DC: National Geographic, 2003.

Faber, Harold, ed. *Luftwaffe: A History.* New York: Quadrangle-*New York Times,* 1977.

Heppenheimer, T. A. *A Brief History of Flight*. New York: John Wiley, 2001.

*Josephy Jr., Alvin M., ed. *The American Heritage History of Flight*. New York: American Heritage, 1962.

*Kane, Joseph Nathan. *Famous First Facts*. New York: H. W. Wilson, 1963.

*Lindbergh, Charles A. *The Spirit of St. Louis*. New York: Scribner, 1953.

Mitchell, William. *Skyways*. Philadelphia: Lippincott, 1930.

Oughton, Frederick. *Aces*. New York: Putnam, 1960.

*Rinard, Judith E. *Book of Flight*. Buffalo, NY: Firefly Books, 2001.

Roseberry, C. R. *Glenn Curtiss: Pioneer of Flight*. Syracuse, NY: Syracuse University Press, 1972.

Solberg, Carl. *Conquest of the Skies: A History of Commercial Aviation in America*. Boston: Little, Brown, 1975.

*Wilson, Mitchell. *American Science and Invention*. New York: Bonanza, 1960.

*Recommended for younger readers

Index

Page numbers for illustrations are in **boldface**.

About the Author

Harold Faber, a retired newspaper reporter and editor at *The New York Times,* was trained as an army air corps aircraft mechanic in World War II. Later, as a war correspondent for the *Times* in Korea, he wrote often about the air force in combat. He is also the author and editor of many books on politics and history, including *Luftwaffe: A History,* the story of the rise and fall of the German air force in World War II.